Happy Entertaining
Ruth Macpherson

THAT'S
ENTERTAINING

RUTH MACPHERSON

HAMMOND®
INCORPORATED
MAPLEWOOD, NEW JERSEY 07040

Cover Photo:
Foreground: Cheese Boat, Page 151
Rear: Pineapple Shrimp Appetizers with Dip, Page 128

Printed in the United States of America.

Library of Congress Cataloging in Publication Data

Macpherson, Ruth.
    That's entertaining.

    Includes index.
    1. Entertaining.   2. Menus.   I. Title.
TX731.M27   642   81-4275
ISBN 0-8437-3377-2   AACR2

CONTENTS

INTRODUCTION

If you are looking for delicious, easy and different recipes for your next party, *That's Entertaining* is the perfect book for you. More than a collection of recipes, it includes party menus and offers shortcuts and hints to make your entertaining easier and more fun.

The first part of the book deals with the Cocktail Party; the second presents Brunch, Lunch and Dinner Party menus and recipes for from four to twelve guests. The last section, Large Parties for Special Occasions, includes menus that will serve sixteen or more. You can just as easily entertain a large number of guests if you do all the work ahead of time and keep your menu simple and sensible.

Most of the recipes can be prepared ahead and just need to be reheated or taken from the refrigerator at the last minute. As you will notice, practically all the recipes are for from eight to twelve people, but can easily be doubled or tripled for more guests. And do not be afraid of a few of the recipes for larger servings. For instance, do not pass up the wonderful Large Brie in Pastry because it serves twenty-four people and you are having only sixteen guests. Cut down on other foods and either freeze the leftover Brie or refrigerate and cut off wedges for snacks or lunch.

To have a successful party, you need to feel confident in yourself so that you can turn your attention to your guests when they arrive. You want to enjoy their company, and you want to have a good time too. A sure way to have this confidence is to plan your party carefully. Make out lists, and don't leave anything for the last minute. Knowing you have taken care of all the details will give you the assurance you need to enjoy the party as much as your guests will.

Remember the time you had a party where everyone else brought the food or the time you were extravagant enough to have it catered (or wished you had)? I'll bet the party was a tremendous success, and I'll bet you thought how easy it was and what a great time you had! How would you like to give a party and know ahead that you are going to enjoy it every bit as much as your guests? *That's Entertaining* will give you all kinds of tips on hassle-free entertaining for small and large gatherings.

From years of experience working with hostesses to prepare for both small and large gatherings, I have discovered that the same questions about entertaining keep popping up. Hopefully you will find answers to some of your own questions in the shortcuts and hints which will be found in the next few pages and at the beginning of each section.

Getting Organized—Planning Makes Perfect

Take time to plan your party with lists. Less hassle—more accuracy!

GUESTS: Keep this list by the phone so you can write down all acceptances or regrets.

MENU: Make shopping lists from this. Include lots of parsley.

BAR: Add lemons, soda, mixers, liquor, and ice to your shopping list if necessary.

RENTALS: Check your supply of china, glassware, silverware, serving trays, salt and pepper shakers, and linen well in advance. List any items you may need to rent or borrow.

PAPER PARTY GOODS & DECORATIONS: Choose candles, doilies, cocktail napkins, dinner napkins, toothpicks, etc., which will complement your party decorating scheme. Should you plan to have fresh flowers for decoration, check with your florist as to what will be available and reasonable in cost. And don't overlook your own garden if you should be lucky enough to have one.

HELP: If you are planning an especially elegant occasion or if your guest list is very long, you may wish to engage outside help. For a party of twenty or more, someone in the kitchen who can watch the stove and oven and do the dishes is invaluable. Get a professional waitress or capable teenager.

COOKING & SERVING: Note oven temperatures and all cooking times. Set out serving bowls and platters. Tape a note on each one about the food to be served in it and how it is to be garnished.

Once you have made your lists, take a few minutes to read again these useful tips. They will help you in that most important aspect of entertaining—planning and preparation.

■ Written invitations save you a lot of time on the phone.

■ If your party is built around a special event, it may provide the inspiration for your choice of table settings and centerpiece, and for those candles and paper goods which you may have to purchase. The degree of formality of your party will also dictate your choice of decorations and serving pieces.

■ Take the weather into consideration. If it's beastly hot, try serving a cold meal. For a chilly tailgate party, a tempting hot drink or soup would be especially appealing.

■ When preparing your grocery list, be sure to check for ingredients that you *think* you have in the refrigerator or cabinet—for example, vanilla, nuts, garlic, flour, etc. Save yourself the frustration of discovering that the flour bag in the cabinet is almost empty!

■ For a large party—or, for that matter, any party where guests are not seated at tables but will be using chairs, steps, floors, etc.—serve foods that will require a fork only.

■ Reserve dishes that require last-minute cooking for those occasions when you are entertaining a small number of people.

■ Be sure to take into account your oven and stove-top capacity. If you are short on oven space, for example, plan to include a hot dish that can be heated on top of the stove, or plan to use more cold foods. Wherever possible, do the cooking ahead. The time needed for reheating will be less than as though you started from scratch on the day itself.

■ When doubling a recipe, do not double-salt—*taste first.*

■ If a dish is too salty, try adding a peeled raw potato and cook for a few minutes.

■ One pound of uncooked shrimp in shells yields about a half pound by the time it is cooked and cleaned.

■ Some types of commercially grown fresh produce such as cucumbers are coated with wax and must be peeled. Homegrown fruits and vegetables need not always be peeled. If you wish to leave them whole because of their color appeal, the skins may be scored with the tines of a fork or scalloped.

■ Phyllo dough—which is used in a number of recipes in this book—can be purchased fresh in specialty food shops or frozen in supermarkets. Fresh dough is easier to work with than frozen and will keep about six weeks in the refrigerator. When you buy a package, check the inside plastic sleeve; you will be able to see if there is any mold (too old!). The edges of the leaves should be smooth, not flaky. Thaw frozen phyllo in the refrigerator a day before using. Have plenty of melted butter, a sharp knife, and a good pastry brush on hand. It is essential that the pastry not dry out, so keep it covered with plastic wrap or waxed paper and a dampened towel. As you work, brush quickly and thoroughly with melted butter. If you take these precautions, you'll find that recipes made with phyllo dough are relatively simple to prepare.

■ Good flavored bread crumbs can be made by whirling your favorite commercial stuffing mix in a blender or food processor. Crusts and ends of bread loaves make good unflavored bread crumbs.

■ When you start work on a recipe, it helps to have all the ingredients set out on the counter.

■ Make sure you have the proper utensils set out beforehand. Special items, such as popover pans or a deep fryer, may be stored at the back of the closet.

■ Know your stove. Most household ovens are inaccurate by at least a few degrees. Rely on an oven thermometer rather than the temperature dial.

■ Know your cookware. Food cooks faster in glass containers. When baking in glass cookware, turn the oven down by 25°. If a recipe calls for baking at 350° for 30 minutes, bake at 325° for 30 minutes. Shiny metal containers, on the other hand, reflect heat and may therefore require longer cooking time.

■ If you are cooking more than one casserole, fillet, etc., in your oven at one time, the cooking time will be a little longer.

■ Keep a few 2- or 3-quart oven-proof glass dishes handy. They're useful for baking, and inexpensive as well. They can fit into silver troughs (which you can rent for very little) or into straw containers.

■ You may find it desirable to prepare more food than you need for the party you have planned. The unused portion can be kept in one of those handy glass dishes and stored in the freezer for future use. Some of the recipes in this book make excellent and unusual gifts. For example, fill a mayonnaise jar with Shrimp Fondue or beer-flavored cheese dip. Put a square of pretty fabric over the closed lid and tie it with a matching yarn ribbon. Put the boat and the bread cubes in plastic bags and tie them with the same ribbon. Or pack Roasted Pecans in an apothecary jar.

■ For easy removal of molded dishes, rinse inside of mold with cold water, drain, then spray with a vegetable oil. Your molded dessert or aspic will look shiny and come out easily. Invert the mold on a platter, lift it a little on one side, and run a grapefruit knife around the edge if necessary to get it started.

■ Make use of decorative bowls, dishes, and baskets. We all like to see pretty things—use your imagination. For instance, an unusually shaped or old basket with a bright napkin and a pretty bowl can hold your bread-sticks, rolls, or silverware. A treasured crystal bowl will look lovely filled with Belgian carrots or cookies.

■ Have plenty of fresh parsley on hand for decorating. Arrange it on trays with hors d'oeuvres, sprinkle on casseroles just before serving, and remember, a bite is good for your breath!

■ Whenever possible, set out split and buttered rolls on your buffet table. It's easier for your guests, and individual spreading will only hold up others who are waiting. You may prepare the rolls, wrap them in aluminum foil, and freeze them. Just thaw them before the party and heat them in the foil.

■ Do not worry about your house being perfect. Large crowd or small, your guests are more interested in you and the other guests and in your good food!

■ Consider the lighting of your cocktail or dinner party. Set candles and softly gleaming oil lamps around the room. Dim the overhead lights, if possible, to help create a cheerful, relaxed mood.

■ Use your timer and don't be afraid to join your guests with one in your pocket.

■ If you relax, smile, and have a good time, your guests can't help but have a good time too. It's contagious.

COCKTAIL
PARTIES

■ When planning your hors d'oeuvres, a good rule of thumb is to count on three or four per person per drinking hour before dinner, and about ten per person for a two-hour cocktail party. Remember, guests are a lot hungrier on a Friday evening than on a Sunday afternoon.

■ Keep in mind the size of your cocktail party when planning the food. For a large party, finger food passed on a serving tray will be more convenient, since guests will be holding a drink and maybe a purse or cigarette. Place dips, spreads, molds and cheeses on a table. There is less chance of something dripping or accidentally spilling. If possible, set food out at a few strategic spots—on a glass-topped server or a cocktail table. The objection to one large table laden with good food is that the people standing around it usually feast while guests in other rooms may not even see the spread.

■ Keep your bar in an open, easily accessible area. A small room with a narrow entrance can be difficult to reach.

■ When passing hors d'oeuvres, start from different parts of your house so that the people in remote places see a fresh tray, too.

■ Paper doilies are a nice touch on hors d'oeuvre trays. Keep the size of your trays to around 14″ since they can become very heavy when passing. Set larger trays on a table.

■ Make sure you have plenty of ice. If you have a storage problem, think of the clothes washer—it's clean, has a drain, and is more insulated than a bathtub!

■ Buy plenty of cocktail napkins. You need them for drinks and for hors d'oeuvres. If the weather is hot, use two for each glass.

■ You can't have too many ashtrays and coasters scattered about on tables, etc.

■ Don't feel shy about asking a guest to pass a tray (especially if he or she doesn't know anyone). The guest is usually only too happy to help. It is also a good way for people to mix.

■ The local liquor dealer can help you to decide what and how much to order for a party, and he will often take back whatever is unopened. Don't forget to stock plenty of mixers and soft drinks.

■ Tape a list to the refrigerator door showing what is to be served and how it is to be prepared.

■ Use name tags if a large number of your guests do not know each other.

■ If you want to end your party (for any number of reasons), just stop serving food and put away the bottles.

■ Instead of having an open bar, try serving a punch or just wines—guests like a little surprise! But be careful. We had a Fishhouse Punch Party a few years ago around Christmas, and we are still holding, unclaimed, a beaded purse and three unmatched shoes.

IMPROMPTU COCKTAILS

■ ■

4–6 people   * Do Ahead

Cold: * Cucumber Appetizers
        * Crab and Caviar Dip
Hot: * Cheese en Croûte

Last-minute invitations. You have been at the pool or a
meeting and you blurted out impulsively, "How about coming over to my place for cocktails tonight?" Well, you did it,
they are coming, and now you want your food to look and
taste as if you meant your invitation, but you've only got an
hour or so to get it all together.

CUCUMBER APPETIZERS

6 servings

A very refreshing taste.

2 3-ounce packages chive
  cream cheese

¼ cup chopped stuffed
  green olives
3 cucumbers, peeled

Halve cucumbers lengthwise and scoop out seeds with a spoon or corer. Combine cheese and olives and fill hollows with mixture. Press halves together, wrap tightly in plastic wrap, and chill. Cut crosswise into ½-inch slices and serve.

CRAB AND CAVIAR DIP

6 servings

Guests cannot quite figure out what it is, but they sure like it. They are always surprised to learn how easy it is to make. Good with carrot sticks, plain crackers, or shredded wheat crackers.

1 6-ounce box frozen Alaska
  king crab or snow crab meat
1 cup sour cream

1 2-ounce jar red caviar
1 teaspoon of lemon juice

Thaw crab according to package directions, drain, and shred. Mix with remaining ingredients and chill.

15

CHEESE EN CROÛTE

6 servings

This is the greatest. Nothing could be simpler, and all but the baking can be done ahead.

½ 8-ounce tube refrigerated
crescent rolls

1 7-ounce Edam or Gouda
cheese

1 teaspoon mustard,
preferably Dijon-style

1 egg, beaten
sesame seed

Remove 4 rolls and place on small cookie sheet. Arrange 2 of the 4 rolls next to the other 2 rolls to form a rectangle approximately 5″ x 7½″. With fingers, smooth out perforated marks on dough to form solid rectangle. Press dough to enlarge rectangle to approximately 6″ x 8″. Remove casing from cheese and place cheese in center of dough. Coat cheese with mustard and bring up all corners of dough to completely encase cheese, making sure all openings are sealed. Brush top and sides with beaten egg and sprinkle with sesame seed. At this point, the cheese can be refrigerated for several hours.

Preheat oven to 375°. Bake for 20–25 minutes, or until golden. Allow to sit a few minutes before slicing into wedges.

COCKTAILS
BEFORE DINING OUT

6–10 people   * Do Ahead

Cold: * Marinated Shrimp
         * Cream Cheese with Cucumber
           Relish and Crackers
Hot: * Oysters and Bacon

What a perfect occasion to serve these tasty, light morsels. The guests have been invited to your place to assemble
before dining out, and you want to serve a drink and something that will perk up their appetites.

MARINATED SHRIMP

Try to get decent-sized shrimp for this spicy dish—the tiny ones just don't make it. There should be about 25–30 shrimp to a pound. I sometimes buy them already cooked and cleaned at the local fish store.

2 medium onions, sliced
1 pound shrimp, cleaned
  and cooked
1 bay leaf, crumbled

Marinade:
  2 teaspoons sugar
  1 teaspoon salt
  ½ teaspoon dry mustard
  2 tablespoons Worcestershire
    sauce
  ¼ cup catsup
  ⅓ cup vinegar
  1 cup salad oil

Soak onion rings in ice water to crisp. Alternate layers of shrimp, drained onion rings, and crushed bay leaf in quart jar. Mix all marinade ingredients until well blended. Pour over layered shrimp, cover, and chill 48 hours. Drain and serve in a pretty silver or glass bowl with toothpicks.

CREAM CHEESE WITH CUCUMBER RELISH

10 servings

Just in case you do not make your own cucumber relish, look for a jar at a delicatessen or food specialty shop. It is a very bright green, and makes an attractive color and flavor contrast with the cream cheese.

1 8-ounce package cream
  cheese

1 8-ounce jar cucumber relish

Place cream cheese on a serving dish. Pour relish over the cheese and serve with crackers.

OYSTERS AND BACON

An all-time favorite in my home. Try to buy refrigerated rather than canned oysters. Make a lot—they go quickly.

bacon slices

oysters

Halve bacon slices and wrap around oyster. Broil on drip pan approximately 3 minutes each side, turning once.

COCKTAILS AND ON TO SOUP AND SANDWICHES

████████████████████████████████████

12 people

* Do Ahead
* * Freeze

Cold: * Broccoli and Carrot Crudités
* Crab Cocktail over Cream Cheese
Hot: * * Hot and Spicy Meatballs
* * Spinach Balls
Soup: * * Cucumber Soup
Sandwiches: Small Store-bought Triple-decker
Party Sandwiches
or
Ham and Cheese Miniatures

Make this an informal Friday- or Sunday-night get-to-gether. You won't even need to use a dining room table for this party. Bring out the hors d'oeuvres before your guests arrive and place them on tables in the living room, den, or porch. The meatballs can be put in a chafing dish over low heat, and the spinach balls can be heated and passed around. Fill mugs with hot soup in the kitchen and pass them on a tray. As for the sandwiches, just stack them on a tray or in a flat basket lined with a pretty cloth placemat. Set the basket and some napkins on a coffee table and let your guests help themselves.

BROCCOLI AND CARROT CRUDITÉS

Approximately 100 pieces

Marinating enhances the bright orange and jade colors of the vegetables.

Carrots:
8 carrots, cut into small sticks
3 tablespoons vinegar
3 tablespoons oil
1 clove garlic, crushed
1 teaspoon seasoned salt
   minced parsley

Broccoli:
1 bunch broccoli, cut into
   bite-size flowerets
¼ cup olive oil
1 teaspoon garlic salt
½ cup sliced stuffed olives
¼ cup lemon juice

Carrots: Put carrot sticks in a plastic bag. Mix other ingredients and pour over carrots. Tie bag and refrigerate overnight.

Broccoli: Put flowerets in another plastic bag. Mix other ingredients well and pour over broccoli. Turn bag around a few times until flowerets are coated. Tie bag and refrigerate overnight.

To serve, drain carrots and broccoli. Pile broccoli in center of platter and surround with carrots.

CRAB COCKTAIL OVER CREAM CHEESE

Approximately 20 servings

This doesn't last very long. Use a shallow soup dish to hold the mixture. Place it in the center of a large platter and surround with crackers. Choose Alaska king crab or snow crab meat for this colorful dish.

2 8-ounce packages cream
   cheese
1 small onion, minced
½ cup mayonnaise
1 tablespoon lemon juice
1 teaspoon garlic salt

1 tablespoon Worcestershire
   sauce
¾ cup chili sauce
2 5-ounce boxes frozen
   crab meat

Bring cream cheese to room temperature. Add next five ingredients and blend well. Shape to fit center of serving plate and cover with plastic wrap. For an easier version, omit mayonnaise and put blocks of cream cheese in a dish and cover with rest of ingredients. Refrigerate overnight. To serve, cover top of mixture with chili sauce, then place shredded drained crab meat on top so that entire surface is covered.

HOT AND SPICY MEATBALLS

Approximately 36 meatballs

Men really go for these meatballs.

Sauce:

¾ cup catsup
½ cup water
¼ cup cider vinegar
2 tablespoons brown sugar
1 tablespoon minced onion
2 teaspoons Worcestershire sauce
1½ teaspoons salt
1 teaspoon dry mustard
¼ teaspoon pepper
3 drops Tabasco

Meatballs:

¾ pound ground beef
¾ cup fine dry bread crumbs
¾ teaspoon salt
½ teaspoon pepper
½ teaspoon monosodium glutamate (MSG)
1½ tablespoons minced onion
½ teaspoon horseradish
3 drops Tabasco
2 eggs, beaten
1 tablespoon butter

Mix sauce ingredients together in bowl and set aside.
Mix all meatball ingredients and shape into ¾-inch balls. Melt butter and brown meatballs in a large skillet in workable batches. In a large pan, place all meatballs, then add sauce. Cover and cook 10 minutes, carefully stirring occasionally. Put into chafing dish and serve with toothpicks.

SPINACH BALLS

Approximately 54 balls

These make a real hit. They may be frozen either before or after baking. If you have frozen them cooked, let them thaw a few hours and bake them just until they are hot—do not overbake or they will dry out.

2 10-ounce packages frozen chopped spinach, thawed and drained well
2 cups herb bread stuffing mix
2 onions, chopped fine
6 eggs, beaten

1½ sticks butter, melted
½ cup grated Parmesan cheese
1 tablespoon garlic salt
½ teaspoon thyme
1 teaspoon monosodium glutamate (MSG)

Preheat oven to 350°.
Mix all ingredients well. Form mixture into balls, using 1 heaping teaspoon mixture for each. Bake on lightly greased baking sheet for 20 minutes.

CUCUMBER SOUP

8 servings

This delicate, pastel soup can be served either hot or cold.

1 bunch scallions, sliced,
 including 1 inch of
 green tops
2 tablespoons butter
4 cups diced cucumbers (2),
 peeled and seeded
3 cups chicken broth

1 cup chopped spinach,
 loosely packed
½ cup sliced potatoes
½ teaspoon salt and pepper
 to taste
 lemon juice
1 cup light cream or milk

Sauté scallions in butter until softened. Add all ingredients except cream and simmer until potatoes are tender, about 10 minutes. Transfer mixture to blender or food processor in batches and puree. Reheat slightly and stir in cream.

If you are serving the soup cold, refrigerate and serve in chilled bowls. Garnish with thin slices of radishes or scallions.

HAM AND CHEESE MINIATURES

20 sandwiches

These delicious little sandwiches can be frozen before they are baked. In addition to being good for a soup and sandwich party, they serve nicely as a hearty hors d'oeuvre. Double the recipe for twelve people.

1 stick butter, softened
2 teaspoons mustard
2 tablespoons poppy seed
2 teaspoons Worcestershire
 sauce
½ onion, grated

1 7½-ounce package party
 or tea rolls
1 4- or 5-ounce package
 sliced cooked ham
1 4-ounce package sliced
 Swiss cheese

Preheat oven to 350°.

Mix butter, mustard, poppy seed, Worcestershire sauce, and grated onion. Open rolls and spread each side with mixture. Top each side with a small piece of ham. Put a small piece of cheese between halves before closing. Bake for 10–12 minutes, or until rolls are crisp and cheese is melted and mixture is bubbly. For a softer sandwich, wrap in aluminum foil and heat.

BRUNCH, LUNCH
AND
DINNER PARTIES

■ When planning your menu, consider the day of the week. Friday-night guests usually eat more (they have not had a chance to nibble), so choose satisfying dishes. Sunday-afternoon guests are usually less hungry (they have been closer to their kitchens), so a lighter menu will be appropriate. On the other hand, Sunday brunch guests will eat up a storm!

■ Do not be afraid to use paper products for any occasion short of an elegant sit-down dinner. Use an imaginative mix of colors for a lovely effect. Just make sure the plates are strong enough to hold the food.

■ Be sensible about your menu selection. Avoid too many fancy or unusual dishes—they might be too much of a good thing. Serve instead one unusual vegetable, potato, or noodle casserole with a "plain" fish, poultry, or meat dish.

■ Make the food look appetizing and think of color contrasts.

> *The good look*—steak, sliced tomatoes, a baked potato, and green beans.

> *The blahs*—creamed chicken, rice, cauliflower, and summer squash.

■ Be careful not to overdo the hors d'oeuvres, particularly when you plan a very special menu. Five per person before dinner are adequate—and you don't have to have that many!

■ Choose types of hors d'oeuvres which will give you maximum time with your guests. For instance, dips, a cheese board, molds, and spreads can be done ahead and placed in a convenient spot. All you have to do is to see that they are passed now and then while you are with your guests—not working in the kitchen.

■ Remember to serve finger foods and those that require only a fork if your guests are not going to be seated at tables.

■ Use foods in season. They are usually a much better buy and of higher quality. Let the time of year be a guideline for your meal.

■ Give special attention to vegetables. They look and taste ever so much better if they are cooked just right—the colors bright and the texture tender-crisp.

■ Take the guesswork out of how much lettuce to buy and prepare for your gathering. A good rule for a buffet is one head of iceberg for eight to ten people. Your salad is also more appealing to the eye when made with different varieties of lettuce. Tear or cut it into small enough pieces to manage easily with a fork. If you are low on cooked dishes, make a little more salad.

■ Become thoroughly familiar with directions for any last-minute cooking, and have all the ingredients ready. Save dishes that require last-minute cooking for smaller parties.

■ Polish the silver and set the table the day before your party. The less you have to do the day of party, the more confident you will feel and act.

■ Seating arrangements for a sit-down: If there are guests of honor, the woman sits at the right of the host; the man, at the right of the hostess. Other guests may be seated as the hostess pleases. If you want to alternate men and women at a dinner for eight, another man should be seated facing the host. Place cards are invaluable. Your guests won't stand around waiting to be directed by you!

■ For a buffet, if you are low on rice and long on chicken, set out the chicken platter first, then the rice. The first dish invariably has more taken from it.

SIMPLY ELEGANT BRUNCH

■■■■■■■■■■■■■■■■■■■■■■■■■■■■■

* Do Ahead
** Freeze

6–8 people

* **Hot Crab Dip**
* **Smoked Salmon and Dill Quiche**
* **Chicken Livers in Wine**
* **Green Salad**
** **Herbed Bread Sticks**
** **Fruit Slush**
* **Bourbon Balls**

This looks like a lot of work, but it's actually quite easy. There is a great deal of food, however, so if you're inviting guests with dainty appetites, you might omit one dish. The dip can be heated ahead and placed in a small heat-proof dish to keep warm. Both the Quiche and the Chicken Livers in Wine can be made a day or two ahead and reheated. The Bourbon Balls should be made well in advance. A simple green salad is a perfect complement for the rich hot dishes. Try Bibb lettuce with a mild dressing.

HOT CRAB DIP

8 servings

No one believes how simple this recipe is. If you want to double it, use only 1½ sticks butter.

1 6½-ounce can white
crab meat

1 8-ounce package
cream cheese
1 stick butter

In a saucepan, combine crab meat, cream cheese, and butter. Heat and mix thoroughly. Transfer to a hot oven-proof dish. Serve with French bread cubes.

SMOKED SALMON AND DILL QUICHE

8–10 servings

This will give you a luxurious result for very little labor. Save yourself a few steps by using a frozen pie crust, and brown it a little before filling. Frozen shells from the supermarket can be thawed and put in your own quiche dish or pie pan before cooking. Quiche can be baked a day or two ahead and then reheated at 350° for 15 minutes, or until hot.

1 10-inch pie shell
½ pound smoked salmon,
chopped
1 cup shredded Swiss cheese
(4 ounces)
4 eggs
1 cup milk
½ cup heavy cream

¼ cup freshly grated
Parmesan cheese
1 tablespoon finely chopped
fresh dill or 1 teaspoon
dried dill weed
½ teaspoon salt
¼ teaspoon pepper
fresh dill for garnish

Preheat oven to 450°.
Pierce pie shell over entire surface with a fork. Bake for 8 minutes, remove to wire rack, and cool slightly.

Spread salmon evenly over bottom of shell. Sprinkle Swiss cheese over salmon. Beat eggs lightly in a medium-size bowl. Add milk, cream, Parmesan cheese, dill, salt, and pepper and mix well. Pour into pie shell.

Bake at 450° for 15 minutes. Lower oven temperature to 350° and bake 15 minutes, or until center is not quite firm. Let stand 15 minutes before serving. Garnish with fresh dill.

CHICKEN LIVERS IN WINE

8 servings

A nice treat for a brunch. Make it a day ahead and reheat gently. Serve in a chafing dish or casserole.

2 large onions, chopped
4 tablespoons butter
24 chicken livers
   all-purpose flour
   salt and pepper

1 pound mushrooms, halved
1 cup chopped cooked ham
   (or fried chopped bacon)
1 cup chicken stock
1 cup dry red wine

Sauté onions in butter until lightly browned. Cut chicken livers in half, roll in flour seasoned with salt and pepper, and cook in the same pan for 4 minutes. Remove chicken livers. In same pan, sauté mushrooms and ham lightly. Stir in 1 teaspoon of the seasoned flour. Cook until brown. Slowly add the stock and wine. Return chicken livers to pan and simmer, uncovered, for 3 minutes.

HERBED BREAD STICKS

96 sticks

These are great for any occasion. Keep several weeks in a sealed container or months in the freezer.

1½ loaves firm white bread,
   sliced very thin
2 sticks butter, softened
2 teaspoons parsley
1 teaspoon chives

1 teaspoon tarragon
1 teaspoon marjoram
1 teaspoon garlic salt
3 tablespoons sesame seed,
   toasted

Preheat oven to 250°.

Remove crusts from bread. Combine all remaining ingredients. Spread on bread. Cut each piece of bread into 4 sticks. Bake for 30 minutes, then turn off heat. Leave in oven 40 minutes.

FRUIT SLUSH

6–8 servings

A cold and refreshing finale.

2 oranges
2 lemons
1 cup sugar
3 bananas, mashed

2 cups ginger ale
1 16-ounce can crushed
   pineapple

Grate the rinds of 1 orange and 1 lemon. Squeeze the juice from the oranges and lemons. Combine juice with remaining ingredients, including rind. Pour into a 6-cup ring mold and freeze. Remove from mold and thaw 20–30 minutes before serving.

BOURBON BALLS

36 balls

Rich and wonderful. Make at least one week before serving and keep in an airtight container in a cool dark place.

½ cup chopped raisins
¼ cup Bourbon whiskey
2 cups chocolate wafer
   crumbs
½ cup dark-brown sugar,
   firmly packed
½ cup finely chopped pecans

¼ cup molasses
½ teaspoon cinnamon
½ teaspoon ginger
¼ teaspoon cloves
   finely chopped pecans for
   coating

In a small bowl, soak raisins in Bourbon for 15 minutes. In a large bowl, combine all ingredients except chopped pecans. Mix well. Form into 1-inch balls and roll them in the pecans to coat well.

EASY DO-AHEAD BRUNCH

10 people

* Do Ahead
** Freeze

* **Cream Cheese Surprises**
* **Company Baked Eggs**
** **Cinnamon Puffs**
** **Quick Blueberry Muffins**
* **Cold Fruit Compote**

Except for cooking the Company Baked Eggs, there is very little you will have to do on the day of the party. Line a basket with a large bright napkin and fold it over the warm Cinnamon Puffs and Quick Blueberry Muffins.

CREAM CHEESE SURPRISES

30 pieces

These savory little filled biscuits are extremely easy to make. They can be assembled, put on a cookie sheet, and refrigerated until ready to bake.

1 8-ounce tube refrigerated
   buttermilk biscuits

1 3-ounce package chive
   cream cheese

Preheat oven to 350°.

Separate biscuits and cut each one into 3 even pieces. Cut chive cheese into 30 pieces. Put cube of cheese on each piece of biscuit, and press dough all around to enclose cheese and form small ball. Bake on ungreased cookie sheet 15 minutes, or until brown.

COMPANY BAKED EGGS

10 servings

An excellent combination for brunch. Cook the sausage and mushrooms and prepare the cheese and tomatoes the day before.

1 pound sweet Italian sausage
1 tablespoon butter
¼ pound mushrooms, sliced
1 medium-size red onion,
   chopped
12 eggs, beaten
1 cup milk
8 ounces mozzarella cheese,
   shredded

2 tomatoes, peeled and
   chopped
½ teaspoon salt
½ teaspoon freshly ground
   pepper
½ teaspoon oregano

Preheat oven to 400°.

Remove casings and crumble sausage into skillet. Fry, stirring constantly, until sausage is no longer pink. Drain well. Clean the skillet, then in it melt the butter. Add mushrooms and onion and sauté until onion is soft. Add drained sausage and all remaining ingredients and mix thoroughly. Turn into a shallow 3-quart baking dish. Bake for 30–35 minutes, or until eggs do not wobble when you carefully shake the dish.

CINNAMON PUFFS

24 miniature muffins

The aroma and flavor of these little biscuits will remind you of cinnamon dough-nuts.

Batter:

⅓ cup butter, preferably unsalted
½ cup sugar
1 egg
1½ cups all-purpose flour
1½ teaspoons baking powder
¼ teaspoon salt
¼ teaspoon nutmeg
½ cup milk

Coating:

⅓ cup sugar
1 teaspoon cinnamon
4 tablespoons butter, melted

Preheat oven to 350°.
Batter: Place butter, sugar, and egg in food processor or blender and mix thoroughly. In a bowl, sift together flour, baking powder, salt and nutmeg. Add dry ingredients and milk alternately to batter. Fill greased miniature-muffin tins two-thirds full. Bake for 20–25 minutes, or until golden brown. Coating: Combine sugar and cinnamon. Roll hot muffins in melted butter, then in cinnamon-sugar mixture. Freeze in aluminum foil.
To serve, thaw the muffins in the foil. Preheat oven to 350°. Heat 10–15 minutes, or until piping hot.

QUICK BLUEBERRY MUFFINS

12 muffins

Sour cream provides tang and a melting texture.

¼ cup sugar
2 cups Bisquick
1 cup sour cream

2 eggs, lightly beaten
1 cup blueberries

Preheat oven to 425°
Combine sugar and Bisquick. Combine sour cream and eggs and add to dry ingredients. Fold in berries. Fill greased muffin cups three-quarters full and bake for 20 minutes.

COLD FRUIT COMPOTE

10 servings

Very good with eggs and poultry. Be sure to bake this the day before.

1 1-pound can dark pitted sweet cherries
1 1-pound can sliced peaches, drained
1 12-ounce package dried apricots
½ cup orange juice
¼ cup lemon juice
1 tablespoon grated orange peel
1 tablespoon grated lemon peel
¾ cup light-brown sugar, firmly packed

Preheat oven to 350°.

Turn cherries and juice into a 1½-quart oven-proof casserole. Add peaches, apricots, orange and lemon juices and peels. Sprinkle with brown sugar. Bake covered for 1½ hours. Cool slightly. Refrigerate overnight.

HEARTY BRUNCH

12 people

* Do Ahead
** Freeze

* Fried Brie
* Brunch Casserole
* Hot Curried Fruit
* Lettuce and Onion Salad with Blue
  Cheese Dressing
** Lemon Crunch Bundt Cake
** Coconut Oatmeal Cake

This is a very easy do-ahead menu. Appetites are usually sharp at brunch, so have plenty of food. A big pitcher of Bloody Marys will go well with this. The Fried Brie is enough for an hors d'oeuvre. All the hot dishes in this meal can be warmed and can then "sit" for a while for late guests or for second helpings.

FRIED BRIE

8–10 servings

Easy, good, and who doesn't love Brie! Place a few clusters of red and green grapes along with the French bread. You will like the melted center and the crunchy crust. Cheese will become firm as it cools, so have a spreader on your serving dish. Make two rounds for twelve to sixteen people.

1 round 8-ounce Brie cheese
all-purpose flour
1 egg
1 tablespoon water
½ cup fine dry bread crumbs, plain or herb-flavored

2 tablespoons butter
½ loaf French bread, cut into cubes

Remove paper and plastic wrappings from cheese. Coat all surfaces with flour. Beat egg with water in a pie plate until foamy. Dip cheese in egg, then in crumbs, coating well. Heat butter in a small skillet just until it foams. Add Brie. Cover and cook over low heat about 5 minutes, or until golden brown on one side. Turn and cook, covered, until bottom is golden brown. Remove from heat. Place on a serving dish and make a cut in the cheese so it will run. Serve at once with the bread cubes.

BRUNCH CASSEROLE

12 servings

A very hearty and tasty dish. Make it the day before if you wish. Reheat the casserole until just warm. Lengthy cooking will dry it out. This dish looks especially nice in a pottery or enamel casserole.

12 hard-cooked eggs, cut into round slices
salt and pepper
1 pound hot bulk sausage, crumbled
1 pound regular bulk sausage, crumbled

3 cups sour cream
1 cup fine dry bread crumbs
2 tablespoons melted butter
3 cups grated Cheddar cheese

Preheat oven to 350°.
Place eggs in buttered oven-proof casserole and season to taste. Cook and drain sausage. Sprinkle sausage over eggs. Spread sour cream over sausage. Toss crumbs with melted butter. Combine crumbs and cheese. Sprinkle over casserole. Bake for 20 minutes, or until heated through.

HOT CURRIED FRUIT

12 servings

This goes so well at a brunch. Heat before your guests arrive and keep warm by covering with dry dish towels.

butter
light-brown sugar
4 bananas
1 29-ounce can pineapple
  chunks
1 29-ounce can sliced peaches

1 29-ounce can apricot
  halves, sliced
1 29-ounce can pear halves,
  sliced
1 16-ounce jar maraschino
  cherries
curry powder

Preheat oven to 350°.
Heavily butter a 13″ x 9″ baking dish and sprinkle with brown sugar. Slice bananas lengthwise and place on bottom. Drain the fruits and layer part of them over the bananas. Sprinkle with curry powder and brown sugar. Repeat layers, omitting bananas. Dot with butter. Bake until bubbly and heated through.

LETTUCE AND ONION SALAD WITH BLUE CHEESE DRESSING

12 servings

A nice combination with very few ingredients.

2 large Bermuda onions
1 3-ounce package blue
  cheese, crumbled
½ cup salad oil
2 tablespoons lemon juice

salt and pepper to taste
½ teaspoon sugar
2 heads lettuce, torn into
  bite-size pieces

Cut onions into thin slices, separate into rings, and place in a bowl. Combine remaining ingredients except lettuce and pour over onion rings. Chill for several hours. Just before serving, toss lettuce with onion mixture.

LEMON CRUNCH BUNDT CAKE

12–16 servings

This crunchy, very lemony cake goes a long way. It takes hardly any time to prepare, especially if you grind the nuts and coconut in a food processor.

1 18½-ounce package
yellow cake mix
1 3¾-ounce package lemon
instant pudding and
pie filling
½ cup oil
1 cup water
1 tablespoon grated lemon
rind

4 eggs, beaten
½ cup flaked coconut
½ cup ground walnuts

Glaze:

⅓ cup lemon juice
2½ cups sifted powdered
sugar

Preheat oven to 350°.

Put cake mix and pudding mix into a bowl. Add oil, water, and lemon rind and mix well. Stir in eggs and blend well. Heavily butter a 10-inch Bundt pan and sprinkle bottom and sides with the ground coconut and nuts (most will settle to the bottom). Pour batter into pan. Bake for 55 minutes, or until toothpick comes out clean. Cool completely.

Glaze: Combine lemon juice and powdered sugar and mix well. Drizzle over cake.

COCONUT OATMEAL CAKE

12–16 servings

Ideal for any occasion and can be served right from the pan.

1½ cups boiling water
1 cup quick-cooking oatmeal
1½ cups all-purpose flour
1 teaspoon cinnamon
1 teaspoon baking soda
½ teaspoon salt
1 cup brown sugar, firmly packed
1 cup white sugar
2 eggs, lightly beaten
½ cup salad oil

Topping:
1 cup brown sugar, firmly packed
½ cup evaporated milk
1 stick butter
1 teaspoon vanilla
½ cup chopped walnuts
¾ cup flaked coconut

Preheat oven to 350°.

Pour boiling water over oatmeal and set aside. Sift together flour, cinnamon, baking soda and salt. Combine sugars, eggs, and oil and add dry ingredients. Add moistened oatmeal and mix well. Pour into a greased and floured 13″ x 9″ pan. Bake 40–45 minutes. Remove from pan and let cool on a rack.

Topping: In a saucepan, dissolve sugar in milk. Add butter. Cook, stirring constantly, until mixture boils and becomes thick. Remove from heat and add vanilla, nuts, and coconut. Pour over cake while sauce is still warm.

A SEAFOOD ENTREE LUNCHEON

6–8 people

* Do Ahead
* * Freeze

* **Curried Beef Dip with Raw
     Vegetables and Crackers**
* * **Shrimp Tetrazzini**
* **Gazpacho Salad with Asparagus**
* * **Buttered Rolls**
* **Chocolate Whiskey Cake**

A great luncheon for any season of the year. The hors
d'oeuvres are made a day or two ahead in the same dish
used for serving. The Shrimp Tetrazzini uses many pots and
pans but is well worth the clean-up. The Gazpacho Salad is
unmolded, garnished with asparagus and lemon wedges,
and kept in the refrigerator until ready to serve. The rolls
can be split, buttered, and wrapped any time and either
refrigerated or frozen.

CURRIED BEEF DIP

8 servings

A very tasty and easy last-minute hors d'oeuvre. Goes well with crackers and raw vegetables such as celery, carrots, cauliflower, mushrooms, etc.

1 8-ounce package cream cheese, at room temperature
2 tablespoons milk
½ cup sour cream
2½ ounces dried beef, chopped
2 tablespoons finely chopped onion

2 tablespoons finely chopped green pepper
⅛ teaspoon pepper
1½ teaspoons curry powder
⅓ cup chopped walnuts, pecans, or peanuts

Blend cream cheese and milk until smooth. Add sour cream and mix well. Add remaining ingredients except nuts and mix well. Spoon mixture into shallow oven-proof serving dish. Sprinkle with chopped nuts. Cover and refrigerate.

Preheat oven to 350°. Bake uncovered for 20 minutes.

If you are using raw vegetables as accompaniments, they can be prepared ahead and refrigerated until ready to serve.

SHRIMP TETRAZZINI

8 servings

Your kitchen will be filled with the tantalizing aromas of Italian food as you whisk together broth, clam juice, wine, and herbs for this very special sauce. The amount of shrimp can vary, but the best is bought fresh, then cooked and peeled. Depending on the size, you may wish to halve the large ones.

1 stick butter
1 bunch scallions, sliced, including 1 inch of the green tops
½ cup cold water
5 tablespoons all-purpose flour
2½ cups chicken broth
½ cup dry white wine
½ cup clam juice
½ cup heavy cream

½ teaspoon oregano
½ cup freshly grated Parmesan cheese
2 tablespoons vegetable oil
2 cloves garlic, peeled and split
12 ounces mushrooms, sliced thin
12 ounces spaghetti
2 pounds shrimp, cooked and shelled
salt

Melt half the butter in a heavy saucepan. Add scallions and water. Bring to a boil, reduce heat to moderate, and cook until all water has boiled away. Stir in flour and cook about 3 minutes; do not brown. Add broth, wine, clam juice, cream, and oregano. Cook, whipping constantly with a whisk, until sauce comes to a boil. Stir in half the cheese. Remove from heat and set aside.

Melt remaining butter with oil in skillet. Add garlic and mushrooms and sauté until mushrooms are brown. Remove from heat and discard garlic. Boil spaghetti al dente. Drain well.

Combine sauce, mushrooms, spaghetti, and shrimp; add salt to taste. Pour into greased 13" x 9" casserole and sprinkle with remaining cheese. Cover and refrigerate.

Preheat oven to 375°. Bake uncovered for 20 minutes, or until bubbly.

GAZPACHO SALAD WITH ASPARAGUS

8 servings

This is a tangy, vegetable-flecked mold, a good accompaniment to the Mediterranean flavors of the casserole.

2 envelopes unflavored
  gelatin
1 18-ounce can tomato juice
⅓ cup wine vinegar
1 teaspoon salt
  dash Tabasco
2 medium tomatoes,
  peeled and diced

1 large cucumber,
  peeled and diced
1 green pepper, diced
¼ cup finely chopped
  red onion
1 tablespoon chopped chives
2 pounds asparagus, cooked
  lemon wedges

In a saucepan, sprinkle gelatin over ½ cup of the tomato juice. Dissolve over low heat and add vinegar, salt, Tabasco, and the remaining juice. Chill until consistency of egg white. Fold in tomatoes, cucumber, pepper, onion, and chives. Pour into a 6-cup mold which has been rinsed with cold water and sprayed with vegetable oil. To serve, unmold on a large platter and garnish with asparagus and lemon wedges.

CHOCOLATE WHISKEY CAKE

8–10 servings

Very rich and delicious. A candied violet in the middle looks lovely.

¼ cup raisins
¼ cup Bourbon
6½ ounces sweet
(dark German) chocolate
½ ounce unsweetened
chocolate
3 tablespoons water
½ cup butter
3 eggs, separated
⅔ cup sugar
¼ cup all-purpose flour
⅔ cup ground almonds
pinch of salt

Frosting:
½ stick butter, melted
3 tablespoons milk
1½ tablespoons unsweetened
cocoa
1¾ cups powered sugar

Preheat oven to 375°.

Steep the raisins in the Bourbon. Butter a 9-inch cake pan and line with wax paper, then butter and flour. Melt chocolate with water in the top of a double boiler and add the butter. Beat egg yolks with the sugar until the mixture is a pale creamy yellow. Combine with chocolate mixture. Mix the flour with the almonds and stir into the chocolate mixture. Fold in raisins and Bourbon. Whip egg whites with a pinch of salt until stiff but not dry. Fold egg whites into the chocolate mixture. Pour into pan. Bake for 20 minutes. Cool for 10 minutes before removing from pan. When cool, top with frosting.

Frosting: Combine all ingredients and beat until smooth. Spread top and sides of cake.

LUNCHEON
FAR FROM THE KITCHEN

8 people

* **Creamy Gazpacho**
* **Cheese Toasts**
** **Rice Casserole with Ham and Broccoli**
* **Raspberry Dream Salad Mold**
** **Buttered Rolls**
* **Meringue Almond Torte**

A luncheon you can be very proud of without spending more than a few minutes in the kitchen.

CREAMY GAZPACHO

Refreshing and different. Chill at least one hour or overnight. Garnish with caviar on a melba round, or with almonds, bacon, or parsley. No cooking!

4 cucumbers, peeled and
cut into large cubes
2 cloves garlic
3 cups chicken broth
3 cups sour cream

3 cups plain yogurt
3 tomatoes, peeled and
chopped
salt and pepper
to taste

Blend cucumbers, garlic, and chicken broth in blender. In a bowl, combine cucumber mixture and sour cream with a whisk. Add yogurt and mix well. Add tomatoes, salt, and pepper. Chill.

CHEESE TOASTS

24 pieces

A nice touch with soup. Have the toasts on a cookie sheet and ready for the oven before your guests arrive.

6 frankfurter rolls
1 stick butter, softened
½ teaspoon seasoned salt

½ teaspoon seasoned pepper
1 cup freshly grated
Parmesan cheese

Preheat oven to 425°.

Cut rolls crosswise in half, then split halves open lengthwise, making 24 pieces. Combine butter, salt, pepper, and cheese. Spread mixture on split sides. Bake for 6–8 minutes.

RICE CASSEROLE WITH HAM AND BROCCOLI

8 servings

A big hit, this casserole may be baked in advance and frozen. You may thaw it and then reheat, or place it in the oven while still frozen and bake for two hours.

1 8-ounce container
   Cheddar cheese spread
2 cans cream of chicken
   soup, undiluted
½ cup milk
½ cup chopped onion
4 tablespoons butter
2 10-ounce packages frozen
   chopped broccoli,
   cooked and drained

4 cups diced ham
2 cups "instant" rice,
   uncooked
½ teaspoon Worcestershire
   sauce

Preheat oven to 350°.

In a large bowl, blend cheese spread, soup, and milk. Sauté onion in butter until tender. Add onion, broccoli, ham, rice, and Worcestershire sauce to soup mixture and mix well. Pour into a 3-quart oven-proof casserole. Bake for 35 minutes. (Frozen: Cover tightly and freeze. Bake covered in preheated 400° oven for 1½ hours. Uncover and continue cooking for 30 minutes more.)

RASPBERRY DREAM SALAD MOLD

8 servings

Goes well with any number of dishes.

1 3-ounce package
   raspberry gelatin
¾ cup hot water
1 10-ounce package frozen
   raspberries, thawed
2 tablespoons sugar

1 cup small-curd
   cottage cheese
1½ tablespoons mayonnaise
½ cup chopped pecans
1 cup heavy cream,
   whipped

Dissolve gelatin in hot water and cool in refrigerator until syrupy. Add berries and sugar. Add cottage cheese, mayonnaise, and pecans. Fold in whipped cream. Pour into 6-cup ring mold which has been rinsed in cold water and sprayed with vegetable oil. Chill. To serve, unmold and surround with leaves of curly lettuce or chicory.

MERINGUE ALMOND TORTE

A foamy, creamy, and crunchy sensation. Made and assembled the day before, this delightful torte is served directly from refrigerator to table.

Meringue Layers:
- 3 egg whites, at room temperature
- ½ teaspoon cream of tartar
- ¾ cup sugar

Topping:
- ½ cup heavy cream
- 2 tablespoons toasted sliced almonds
- whole strawberries

Toasted Almond Filling:
- 3 tablespoons butter, at room temperature
- ½ cup sugar
- ¾ teaspoon almond extract
- 2 egg yolks
- 1 cup toasted finely ground almonds
- ½ cup heavy cream

Meringue: *Preheat oven to 250°.* Trace three 8-inch circles on wax paper or parchment and place on baking sheets. Beat egg whites with cream of tartar until soft peaks form. Gradually beat in ½ cup of the sugar, 2 tablespoons at a time, until mixture is shiny and holds stiff peaks. Gently but thoroughly fold in remaining ¼ cup sugar. Divide and spread evenly over each circle. Bake for 1 hour. Turn heat off, but leave meringues in oven for 3 hours to cool and dry completely. Carefully peel off paper.

Filling: Cream butter and sugar together until light and fluffy. Add almond extract and blend well. Add egg yolks one at a time, beating well after each addition. Stir in almonds. Gradually add cream, beating until mixture is thick.

To assemble: Place a meringue layer on serving platter and spread evenly with half of almond filling. Top with second meringue layer and cover with remaining filling. Place third meringue layer on top. Cover tightly with plastic wrap. Chill at least 18 hours.

Topping: At least 4 hours before serving, lightly whip ½ cup cream and spread over top. Cover and chill. When ready to serve sprinkle with sliced almonds and garnish with strawberries.

ALMOST ALL-COLD LUNCHEON

■ ■

8–10 people

* Do Ahead
** Freeze

* **Large Round Brie in Pastry**
* **Salmon Mousse**
* **Cold Marinated Baby Carrots**
* **Crunchy Tossed Salad**
  Popovers
* **Frosted Orange Slices**
** **Easy Almond Lace Cookies**

A perfect menu for a spring or summer luncheon. The Brie can be baked and ready on a platter when your guests arrive. The mousse is unmolded, garnished, and refrigerated. The carrots have been marinating for days; on the day of your party, just drain, place in a serving dish, and return to refrigerator until ready to serve. The greens are in a salad bowl in the refrigerator ready to be tossed. The popovers will take little time. Have the tins ready, pour in the batter, and pop them in a very hot oven. Carry a timer in your pocket and rejoin your guests. When the bell goes off, luncheon is served!

LARGE ROUND BRIE IN PASTRY

40 servings

Fabulous! What a treat for hungry guests. Make sure the Brie is not too ripe. Thaw commercial frozen pastry for the casing. This should be out of the oven 45 minutes to an hour before serving. Leftover Brie can be frozen.

1 wheel Brie cheese (about 2 pounds)
1 17½-ounce package frozen puff pastry or 2 frozen 9-inch pie shells, thawed
water
1 egg

Preheat oven to 400°.

Roll a sheet of pastry lightly, with as few strokes as possible, to fit bottom and sides and cut to overlap ½ inch on top of Brie. Brush ½″ of pastry rim with water. Roll second sheet of puff pastry very lightly and use top of Brie box to cut dough to exactly fit top. Place on top, using fork to press down and seal edges. Cut out leaves, flowers, or other shapes with any leftover pie crust and decorate top. Mix egg with a little water and brush top. Bake 25 minutes, *or* until crust is golden brown.

Wait 45 minutes to an hour before serving. Cut into thin wedges. Serve surrounded with crackers.

SALMON MOUSSE

10–12 servings

Light and delicious. For color contrast, a circle of thin cucumber slices is attractive along with the fresh dill

2 envelopes unflavored gelatin
⅓ cup cold water or salmon juice
1 cup boiling water
2 tablespoons fresh lemon juice
2 tablespoons vinegar
1 cup heavy cream, whipped
1 cup mayonnaise
½ teaspoon salt
1 medium onion, grated
3 cups canned red salmon, flaked (1-pound can plus 7½-ounce can, approximately)
2 cups chopped peeled cucumbers
3 tablespoons chopped fresh dill
fresh dill for garnish

Soak gelatin in cold water and add to boiling water. Add lemon juice and vinegar. Chill in refrigerator until thick. Add whipped cream to mayonnaise. Combine with chilled mixture. Add remaining ingredients (except dill for garnish) and pour into a large ring mold which has been rinsed with cold water and sprayed with vegetable oil. Chill. To serve, unmold on a round platter and garnish with dill.

COLD MARINATED BABY CARROTS

10 servings

A tangy and colorful vegetable dish. Will keep a week or more refrigerated.

2 16-ounce cans baby
   carrots or 2 pounds
   fresh carrots
1 green pepper, chopped
1 onion, sliced thin
½ cup vegetable oil
1 cup sugar

¾ cup vinegar
1 teaspoon prepared mustard
1 teaspoon Worcestershire
   sauce
1 10¾-ounce can tomato
   soup, undiluted
   salt and pepper

Drain the canned carrots; or, if using fresh carrots, slice and boil until fork-tender. Alternate layers of carrots, green pepper, and onion in a large bowl or jar. Make a marinade of remaining ingredients, beating well until completely blended. Pour mixture over vegetables and refrigerate. Drain and serve.

CRUNCHY TOSSED SALAD

10 servings

Nuts provide unusual flavor and texture. Green spinach and red cabbage make a bright color combination.

1 pound fresh spinach,
   washed, trimmed, and
   dried
½ cup shredded red cabbage
¼ cup unsalted peanuts or
   cashews

Dressing:
1 cup vegetable oil
⅓ cup white vinegar
1 tablespoon minced garlic
1 tablespoon sugar
2 teaspoons paprika
   salt and pepper

Combine spinach, cabbage, and nuts and toss well. Chill until ready to serve.
Dressing: Combine all ingredients in a blender. Refrigerate. To serve, add dressing to taste and toss well.

POPOVERS

These cannot be made ahead, so have all ingredients out and the muffin pans well greased. Guests love them, and they are well worth the last-minute baking. Recipe may be doubled or tripled.

3 eggs
1 cup milk
3 tablespoons butter, melted

1 cup all-purpose flour
½ teaspoon salt

Preheat oven to 425°.

Grease well twelve 2½-inch muffin cups. Beat all ingredients with rotary beater just until smooth. (Overbeating will reduce volume.) Fill muffin cups half full with batter. Bake for 45 minutes. Serve immediately.

FROSTED ORANGE SLICES

A marvelously refreshing citrus combination. Have it ready and refrigerated long enough before your guests arrive so that the serving dish is cold as well as the orange slices. Looks lovely in a glass bowl or arranged in rows on a platter. Do this a day ahead.

16 navel or juice oranges
½ cup fresh lemon juice

grated peel of 4 lemons
⅓ cup sugar

Peel 12 of the oranges, using a very sharp knife. Remove all white membrane. Slice oranges a little less than ½ inch thick. Remove seeds. Place slices in serving dish. In a bowl, combine lemon juice, peel, and sugar. Squeeze remaining oranges and add juice to lemon mixture. Mix well and add to sliced oranges. Turn orange slices a few times, being careful not to break them. Cover and refrigerate at least 4 hours or overnight. Serve chilled, turning once again.

EASY ALMOND LACE COOKIES

Approximately 60 cookies

A crisp and delicate wafer to complement the fresh fruit.

1 cup blanched almonds
1 stick butter, cut up
1 cup sugar

3 tablespoons all-purpose
flour
2 tablespoons milk

Preheat oven to 350°.

Place almonds in food processor and grind fine, using steel blade. Set aside. Put butter in the container with the motor running; slowly add sugar through the tube. Add flour, milk, and ground almonds and blend 3–5 seconds. Transfer to a saucepan and heat the mixture until just hot. Cover cookie sheet with foil and drop the warm mixture on it, using no more than ½ teaspoon per cookie and placing each mound 3 inches apart. Bake 6 minutes, or until lightly browned. Allow to cool slightly, then gently remove with a broad spatula.

QUICK AND EASY DINNER

4–6 people

* Do Ahead
** Freeze

* Quickie Bacon Roll-ups
* Easy Festive Chicken and Rice
* Easy Glazed Carrots
* Quick Herbed Biscuits
** Easy Strawberry Layer Cake
or
** Quick Lemon Yogurt Pie

You need dinner in a hurry—and a nice one. You will find yourself using the chicken not only for company. Your family will love it, too. It is very easy, and it lends itself to preparation for a large group. Fresh cut carrots look particularly nice on the plate with the chicken, adding a touch of bright color. You can also buy canned julienned carrots. Parmesan cheese and herbs make something special of refrigerated biscuits. You will also love having the quick frozen cake and creamy Lemon Yogurt Pie recipes in your collection of instant desserts for any occasion.

QUICKIE BACON ROLL-UPS

12 small appetizers

To make twice as many, use the whole tube of crescent rolls and double the remaining ingredients.

½ 8-ounce tube refrigerated
crescent rolls
¼ cup sour cream

¼ teaspoon seasoned salt
¼ pound bacon, cooked and
crumbled

Preheat oven to 375°
Separate rolls. Combine remaining ingredients and spread on rolls. Cut each into thirds (making triangles) and roll up. Bake 10–12 minutes.

EASY FESTIVE CHICKEN AND RICE

4–6 servings

A wonderful combination. The family will love it, and so will your guests. Can be doubled or tripled easily.

1 6¼-ounce package
fast-cooking long and wild
rice mix with herbs and
seasonings
1 3-pound chicken,
cut into serving pieces
1 16-ounce can whole-berry
cranberry sauce

3 tablespoons butter or
margarine
2 tablespoons soy sauce
1 teaspoon lemon juice
½ cup thinly sliced almonds

Preheat oven to 325°.
Sprinkle rice in buttered 13" x 9" oven-proof casserole. Spread package of seasonings over rice. Arrange chicken, skin side up, on top. In a saucepan, combine cranberry sauce, butter, soy sauce, and lemon juice. Heat, stirring until melted. Pour over chicken. Cover tightly with aluminum foil. Bake for 1 hour and 15 minutes. Uncover, sprinkle with almonds, and bake 10 minutes more. The casserole will keep warm for 30 minutes.

EASY GLAZED CARROTS

6 servings

Fresh carrots with the greens still attached are the best. However, bagged carrots will do.

6 medium carrots, julienned
1 tablespoon butter
1 teaspoon sugar

Steam or boil carrots briefly until just crisp-tender. Melt butter in a small skillet over medium heat. Add carrots, sprinkle evenly with sugar, and toss lightly until heated through.

QUICK HERBED BISCUITS

8–10 biscuits

A great way to pep up supermarket biscuits.

6 tablespoons butter
2 tablespoons Parmesan
   cheese
2 tablespoons parsley flakes
1 tablespoon onion flakes

2 teaspoons celery flakes
1 teaspoon dried dill weed
1 8-ounce tube refrigerated
   biscuits

Preheat oven to 400°.

Melt butter in 8″ x 8″ or 8″ round pan. Sprinkle with seasonings. Top with biscuits. Bake 12–15 minutes. Invert immediately. Serve hot.

EASY STRAWBERRY LAYER CAKE

6 servings

A frozen coconut layer cake may be used for this luscious dessert. Any fresh fruit will do.

1 pint fresh strawberries
1 17-ounce package frozen
   white layer cake

Wash, hull, and halve strawberries. While cake is still frozen, slice into 3 layers. Put bottom layer on a serving dish and top with half the strawberries. Place next layer on top and cover with remaining strawberries, reserving a few for garnish. Place top cake layer on top of strawberries. Decorate top with reserved strawberries. Refrigerate until ready to serve.

QUICK LEMON YOGURT PIE

6–8 servings

Light and wonderful. Does not have to freeze entirely.

2 8-ounce containers
   lemon yogurt

1 8-ounce container frozen
   whipped topping, thawed
1 graham cracker pie crust

Fold yogurt and topping together and spoon into crust. Freeze. Remove from freezer about 15 minutes before serving.

ELEGANT SIT-DOWN DINNER

8 people

* Do Ahead
** Freeze

* Pâté in Gelatin
* Mushrooms Filled with
  Crab Meat
** Carrot Soup
* Spectacular Seafood Strudel
  or
** Chicken Breasts with Duxelles
  in Phyllo Pastry with
  Watercress Sauce
* Seasonal Green Vegetable
* Bibb and Walnut Salad
** Rolls
** Lemon Velvet Mousse
* Chocolate Macaroons

Get out your best linen and polish all your good silver! With this exceptional food, you'll want your very finest to show it off. You will be amazed at how easy this meal really is and how little work you will have to do during your dinner party. The soup should be on the table when your guests sit down. The Lemon Velvet Mousse serves more than eight persons and can be stretched to feed more than twice that number.

PÂTÉ IN GELATIN

Molded in an unusual container, this hors d'oeuvre is a stylish addition to an elegant table. For instance, a mold with a nice design on the bottom (which becomes the top) will result in a clear gelatin layer, a center layer of pâte, and a base of gelatin. I use a mold that produces a flower design of clear gelatin. Use an attractive serving dish and set crackers or a hard pumpernickel bread cut into triangles and lots of parsley around the mold.

1 envelope unflavored
  gelatin
¼ cup cold water
1 4¾-ounce can liver pâté
1 3-ounce package cream
  cheese

2 tablespoons Bourbon
1 10½-ounce can beef
  consommé, heated
2 tablespoons sherry

Mix pâté and cream cheese with Bourbon and set aside. Sprinkle gelatin over cold water. Add very hot consommé to gelatin. Stir in sherry. Pour about a third of the mixture into a small mold which has been rinsed with cold water and sprayed with vegetable oil. Refrigerate for about 20 minutes, or until fairly solid. Spread with pâté mixture and cover with remaining consommé mixture. Refrigerate. Unmold to serve.

MUSHROOMS FILLED WITH CRAB MEAT

Approximately 35 mushrooms

Everyone is wild about these as an hors d'oeuvre, and also as a side dish for steak. As an hors d'oeuvre, medium-size mushrooms are best. There are about 35 to a pound.

1 pound mushrooms, washed and dried	1 6-ounce package frozen king crab meat, thawed
3 tablespoons butter	1 tablespoon Cognac
1 tablespoon all-purpose flour	1 egg yolk
½ cup milk	Tabasco to taste
salt and pepper to taste	¼ cup grated Parmesan or Swiss cheese
½ cup finely chopped scallions, including 1 inch of green tops	4 tablespoons butter, melted

Preheat oven to 400°.

Remove stems from mushrooms, chop, and set aside. Place mushroom caps, hollow side down, in a buttered baking dish. Brush with 1 tablespoon melted butter and bake 10 minutes.

Make white sauce of 1 tablespoon of the butter, 1 tablespoon flour and ½ cup milk. Stir until thickened and add salt and pepper.

Sauté scallions and chopped mushroom stems in remaining 2 tablespoons butter for 4 minutes. Add flaked crab meat and Cognac, mixing well. Add white sauce, egg yolk, and Tabasco. Cook gently until mixture holds together well.

Stuff mushroom caps. Sprinkle with cheese and brush with melted butter. Bake 15–20 minutes at 400°.

CARROT SOUP

A delicious thick soup which is easy to prepare and always brings compliments. Top with chives, parsley, or grated lemon rind. Serve at the table or pass in mugs while guests are still standing at the end of the cocktail hour.

12 medium carrots, diced
2 medium onions, chopped
2 bay leaves
4½ cups chicken stock
6 tablespoons unsalted butter

4 tablespoons all-purpose flour
2 cups milk
salt and pepper

Simmer carrots, onions, and bay leaves for 20 minutes in chicken stock. Discard bay leaves and puree soup in blender or food processor. Melt butter in saucepan, add flour and cook 3 minutes. Stir in puree and cook 3 minutes more. Remove from heat and stir in milk. Season with salt and pepper.

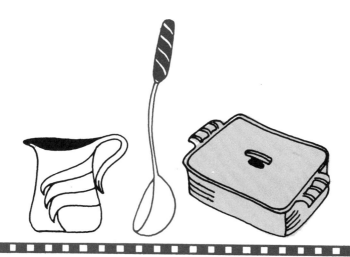

SPECTACULAR SEAFOOD STRUDEL

Prepare this the day before. It really is not hard, and the rewards are worth the labor because it looks fantastic on a silver tray at the head of the table or centered on a buffet table. A one-pound box of phyllo dough will be enough for two strudels. You are not using a large amount of seafood, so the dish is not very expensive. The strudel can be cooked, covered with aluminum foil and a towel and kept on a heating tray up to 1½ hours before serving.

Sauce:
- 2 tablespoons unsalted butter
- 2 tablespoons all-purpose flour
- ½ teaspoon Dijon-style mustard
- salt and pepper
- ¾ cup milk, at room temperature
- 2 tablespoons heavy cream

Strudel dough:
- 1½ cups bread crumbs
- ¼ cup freshly grated Parmesan cheese
- ¼ teaspoon dry mustard
- ½ 1-pound package phyllo dough, at room temperature (See p. 7)
- 1 pound unsalted butter

Filling:
- 1 pound shelled, cooked king crab meat, shrimp, lobster, or combination, cut into bite-size chunks
- ½ cup grated Swiss cheese
- 2 hard-cooked eggs, chopped
- ¾ cup sour cream
- ¼ cup chopped parsley
- ¼ cup diced shallots
- 2 tablespoons chopped chives
- 1 large clove garlic, minced
- 2 tablespoons freshly grated Parmesan cheese

Sauce: Melt 2 tablespoons butter in small saucepan over low heat. Stir in flour to make smooth paste and heat gently, stirring constantly, until mixture just begins to bubble. Remove from heat and add mustard and a pinch each of salt and pepper. Slowly stir in milk. Place over medium heat and cook, stirring constantly, until mixture bubbles and thickens. Add cream and taste for seasoning. Cover and chill until very thick (about 2 hours).

Prepare strudel dough: Combine bread crumbs, Parmesan, and dry mustard in a bowl. Melt 1 pound butter. Unroll half of the phyllo leaves contained in the box of phyllo dough. Set one leaf on counter with longest side nearest to you. Cover remaining leaves with wax paper, then a damp towel.

Butter the phyllo leaf and sprinkle lightly with bread crumbs. Stack a second phyllo leaf on top, butter, and sprinkle with bread crumbs. Repeat layers until all the leaves are stacked in front of you.

Fill strudel: Layer seafood evenly on bottom third of phyllo, leaving about 2 inches unfilled on either side. Sprinkle seafood with Swiss cheese and chopped egg. Dot with sour cream. Sprinkle with most of the parsley, shallots, chives, and garlic and dot with chilled sauce.

Roll strudel: Fold the unfilled 2-inch ends in toward center very carefully. Holding in the two ends so they do not flap out, start rolling the filled end up toward the top. Roll up jelly-roll fashion to make a long plump roll. Place seam side down on a jelly-roll pan. Brush top with melted butter and bake. Or cover securely with plastic wrap and refrigerate. If strudel is refrigerated, bring to room temperature before baking.

Preheat oven to 375°. Bake strudel 12 minutes. Remove from oven and brush with butter in pan. Slice diagonally with serrated knife into 1½-inch pieces. Push slices together to reshape loaf. Return to oven and brush 3 more times during baking. Bake 35–40 minutes longer, or until crisp and golden brown. Remove from oven and brush with butter in pan. Wait 10 minutes and transfer to warmed serving platter. Dust with Parmesan and the rest of the minced parsley.

CHICKEN BREASTS WITH DUXELLES IN PHYLLO PASTRY WITH WATERCRESS SAUCE

12 servings

Three steps make this seem more complicated than it is. The dish is fun to make and you do it all ahead of time. Plan on requests for seconds. It's also a delicacy when cold and sliced thin. (A good substitute for the watercress sauce is a package of creamed spinach.)

Duxelles:

- 1 stick butter
- 5 shallots, chopped fine
- 1½ pounds mushrooms, chopped fine
- 2 tablespoons minced parsley

Chicken:

- 6 whole chicken breasts, split, skinned, and boned
- 4 tablespoons olive oil
- 2 sticks butter
- ⅓ cup Cognac
- 12 sheets phyllo dough (See p. 7)

Watercress Sauce:

- ½ bunch scallions, peeled and sliced, including 1 inch of green tops
- 3 tablespoons butter
- 1 small potato, diced
- 2 cups cubed zucchini
- 1 bunch watercress, trimmed
- 1 cup chicken broth

Duxelles: Melt butter and sauté shallots over low heat until soft. Add mushrooms and cook over low heat, stirring occasionally, until all liquid is evaporated and mixture is very dark. Stir in parsley. Refrigerate.

Chicken: Sauté chicken breasts in the oil and 1 stick of the butter in a heavy skillet until lightly browned on each side (about 2 minutes). Remove to a pan or heat-proof dish. Heat and ignite Cognac and pour over chicken breasts. When flames die out, pour off liquid. Melt the remaining stick of butter in a clean saucepan.

Spread a sheet of phyllo dough on a damp cloth or large cutting board, brush with butter, fold in half, and brush again with butter. Put a chicken breast at narrow end; spread with chilled duxelles. Fold sides in over chicken and roll chicken over and over to make a rectangular package. Repeat with remaining chicken. Brush tops with butter. (May be prepared in advance up to this point, wrapped, and refrigerated or frozen. Bring to room temperature before proceeding.)

Preheat oven to 400°. Butter a jelly-roll pan and put chicken packages on it. Try to have edges underneath. Bake for 25–30 minutes, or until puffed and brown. Keep warm. Serve with a thick ribbon of sauce across center of chicken.

Watercress Sauce: Sauté scallions in butter until soft. Add remaining ingredients and cook until potato is tender (about 8 minutes). Pour into blender or food processor. Refrigerate and reheat when ready to use.

BIBB AND WALNUT SALAD

8 servings

Use a clear glass bowl.

3 heads Bibb lettuce, washed and torn into bite-size pieces

1 cup coarsely chopped walnuts, toasted

¾ cup olive oil

6 tablespoons wine vinegar salt and freshly ground pepper

Arrange lettuce in bowl. Sprinkle with walnuts and toss with oil and vinegar. Season to taste with salt and pepper and serve immediately.

LEMON VELVET MOUSSE

12–16 servings

No cooking is needed for this fabulous dessert. You can make it whenever you have time, and it can be frozen for months. It serves more than eight, so you may be able to return some of it to the freezer for a great last-minute dessert for another meal.

1¾ cups crushed vanilla
  wafers
1½ cups sugar
½ cup + 1 tablespoon
  lemon juice

3 cups heavy cream
6 eggs, separated
¼ teaspoon salt

Line bottom of ungreased 9-inch springform pan with 1 cup of the crumbs. Dissolve sugar in lemon juice and stir. Whip cream and refrigerate. Beat egg yolks slightly with salt. Add to lemon mixture and beat thoroughly until thick. Fold in whipped cream. Beat whites until stiff but not dry, and fold into mixture until thoroughly combined. Pour into pan. Top with remaining crumbs. Wrap and freeze. Unmold, rewrap and return to freezer.

Remove from freezer, unwrap, place on serving platter and refrigerate 2½–3 hours before serving. Any leftover mousse can be frozen again, but return it to the freezer before it loses its shape.

CHOCOLATE MACAROONS

Approximately 60 macaroons

Heavier than a chocolate meringue, these macaroons are always appreciated.

1 14-ounce can sweetened
  condensed milk
2 ounces (2 squares)
  unsweetened chocolate
2 cups shredded coconut
1 cup chopped pecans
  (or ½ cup pecans and
  ½ cup raisins)

1 tablespoon strongly
  brewed coffee
1 teaspoon vanilla
⅛ teaspoon salt

Preheat oven to 350°.

Combine milk and chocolate in top of double boiler. Place over boiling water on high heat and stir constantly until mixture thickens (about 5 minutes). Add remaining ingredients and stir to blend. Drop by teaspoonfuls onto generously greased cookie sheet. Bake 10 minutes, watching carefully so they do not burn. Macaroons should have a soft, chewy texture.

DINNER DE LUXE

8 people

* Do Ahead
** Freeze

* **Avocado Mousse**
** **Crab Puffs with Phyllo**
Beef Tenderloin (Fillet of Beef)
with Madeira Sauce
or
* **Tournedos in Puff Pastry**
* **Easy Rice Casserole**
* **Marmalade Carrots**
* **Caesar Salad**
** **Rolls**
* **Company Chocolate Cake**

A very special "money is no object" dinner party. As you read these recipes, you'll see there is very little you have to do in the kitchen after your company arrives. Use your finest tableware, and add an extra touch with place cards and a bright flower tucked into a bow around each napkin.

AVOCADO MOUSSE

8 servings

You may serve this either before dinner with plain water crackers or as a first course on a pretty glass dish with cucumber slices for garnish. A decorative mold enhances the appeal of this mousse.

4 avocados
½ cup mayonnaise
1 tablespoon unflavored gelatin
1 tablespoon fresh lemon juice
1 tablespoon grated onion
1 teaspoon Worcestershire sauce

1 teaspoon salt
½ teaspoon pepper
¼ teaspoon paprika
6 drops Tabasco
6 tablespoons sour cream cucumber slices

Puree avocados in food processor or blender. Add remaining ingredients except sour cream and cucumber. Mix well. Turn into glass serving bowl. Whip sour cream lightly with fork and spread over mousse to prevent discoloration. Garnish with cucumber slices and refrigerate until set.

CRAB PUFFS WITH PHYLLO

24 puffs

These are absolutely wonderful. Save them for a special occasion because they are rather expensive to make. Fresh, canned, or frozen and thawed crab meat may be used, but puffs made with frozen crab cannot be refrozen. King crab is my preference.

2½ tablespoons butter
1 tablespoon finely chopped shallots
2½ tablespoons all-purpose flour
¾ cup milk
1 egg, beaten
½ pound crab meat, shredded

2 teaspoons chopped parsley
2 teaspoons chopped dill
1 teaspoon dry sherry
6 sheets phyllo dough (See p. 7)
melted butter

Melt the 2½ tablespoons of butter, add shallots, and sauté until soft. Add flour and milk and cook, stirring constantly, until thick. Add egg. Continue cooking and stirring until thicker. Remove from heat. Add shredded crab, parsley, dill, and sherry.

Preheat oven to 350°. Cut sausage-shaped bundle of phyllo into 3-inch strips. Unroll 1 strip and brush with butter. Cut strip in half and fold each piece over itself. Place 1 folded strip in bottom of buttered miniature muffin tin. Let edges overhang. Spoon 2 teaspoons of filling in center of second folded-over strip. Bring edges together to enclose filling (looks like a knapsack). Turn filled pastry over and insert, upside down, inside first pastry. Brush with butter. Bring overhanging edges up and gather them together; pinch closed. Bake for 20 minutes.

BEEF TENDERLOIN (FILLET OF BEEF)

Whole tenderloin makes 8–12 servings;
half makes 4–6 servings.

Nothing could be simpler yet more elegant than a juicy, rare fillet of beef, but the roast must be cooked to perfection. Here is a foolproof method if you use a meat thermometer. Don't be surprised when you see how little meat is left when you have trimmed the fillet.

1 whole or half beef
  tenderloin

1 clove garlic
  salad oil or bacon fat

Preheat oven to 425°.

Remove fat and connective tissue from meat. Rub meat all over with cut garlic clove and then with oil. Place on rack in open roasting pan; tuck narrow end under to make the roast evenly thick. Insert meat thermometer into center of thickest part of meat. Bake 45–60 minutes, or until thermometer reaches 140° (rare). The half tenderloin will require 45–50 minutes baking time.

MADEIRA SAUCE:

2 cups

1½ tablespoons butter
1½ tablespoons all-purpose
  flour

2 cups dark beef stock
⅓ cup Madeira wine

Melt butter in heavy saucepan, add flour and cook, stirring constantly, until brown in color. Gradually add beef stock and simmer for 30 minutes. Add wine and bring to a boil. Serve hot over fillet.

TOURNEDOS IN PUFF PASTRY

8 servings

This very elegant entree may be prepared early in the day and refrigerated until cooking time. Tournedos are small steaks cut from completely trimmed beef fillet.

8 tournedos, 1-1½ inches thick
6 tablespoons butter
salt and pepper to taste
12 ounces mushrooms, chopped
¾ cup liver pâté or liverwurst
4 tablespoons sherry (approximately)
2 17½-ounce packages frozen puff pastry, thawed
1 egg, well beaten

Sauté tournedos in 3 tablespoons of the butter for 3 minutes on each side. Season with salt and pepper and cool. Sauté mushrooms in remaining 3 tablespoons butter. Add pâté and sauté until brown. Add enough sherry to bind mixture. Spread a thin layer of pâté mixture on top of each tournedos. Cool again.

Preheat oven to 400°. Unfold thawed puff pastry (4 sheets). With a sharp knife, trim three ½-inch strips from each sheet and set aside. Cut the 4 sheets in half. On a lightly floured board, roll out the 8 sections (enough to package each tournedos). Place one tournedos on each sheet of pastry. Wrap pastry around tournedos, enclosing it completely. Trim top with lattice strips. Brush top with egg. (The tournedos may be prepared to this point and refrigerated.) Bake for 20–25 minutes, or until puffed and brown. Serve as is or topped with Madeira Sauce.

EASY RICE CASSEROLE

8 servings

An easy and excellent rice casserole that can be assembled ahead and refrigerated. The recipe may be doubled or tripled for a larger party.

½ cup chopped onion
3 tablespoons butter
2 cups cooked rice
1 teaspoon salt
½ cup chopped celery
½ cup minced parsley
1 4-ounce can chopped mushrooms, including liquid
2 carrots, grated

Preheat oven to 300°. Sauté onion in butter. Put all ingredients in buttered 2-quart casserole, mixing with two forks. Bake covered for 45 minutes.

MARMALADE CARROTS

So easy and so good. Buy good canned carrots. If you cannot find Belgian baby carrots, look for nugget carrots. You will be amazed at how well these go with meat and chicken dishes. They need no cooking—just heating.

3 15-ounce cans
  Belgian carrots
1 cup orange marmalade

2 teaspoons tarragon
4 tablespoons butter

Heat carrots in liquid from can. In a small saucepan, combine remaining ingredients and heat. Drain carrots and place in serving bowl. Toss gently with hot marmalade mixture.

CAESAR SALAD

8 servings

Always a favorite.

1 small loaf French bread,
  cut into bite-size cubes
1 stick butter
1 clove garlic, minced
1 egg
2 medium heads romaine
  lettuce
¼ cup olive oil
¼ teaspoon salt

  freshly ground pepper
½ teaspoon Worcestershire
  sauce
2 tablespoons lemon juice
¼ teaspoon dry mustard
¼ cup freshly grated
  Parmesan cheese
  anchovies

Sauté bread cubes in butter with the garlic until golden brown. This should be done well in advance. Coddle the egg by boiling it for 1 minute and immersing in cold water. Tear chilled, well-dried lettuce into medium-size pieces, and place in a salad bowl. Combine olive oil, salt, pepper, Worcestershire sauce, lemon juice, and dry mustard and mix thoroughly. Pour over the greens. Break the coddled egg over the greens and toss well. Sprinkle with Parmesan and croutons. Toss again and serve immediately. Garnish with anchovies.

COMPANY CHOCOLATE CAKE

10–12 servings

I made this for Christmas dinner a few years ago for the first time. Now I feel guilty if I make something else—family and friends start requesting it months in advance. The frosting must be made a day ahead—you'll need a candy thermometer. Delicious.

4 extra-large eggs
¾ cup sugar
¾ teaspoon vanilla
6 tablespoons unsweetened cocoa
⅓ cup finely ground almonds, toasted
2 tablespoons plus 2 teaspoons all-purpose flour
1 stick unsalted butter, melted

Chocolate Mousse Frosting:
5 ounces bittersweet chocolate
2 tablespoons milk
1 teaspoon instant coffee powder
2 eggs, separated
⅓ cup sugar
2 tablespoons water
½ cup heavy cream
8–16 ounces bittersweet chocolate, grated

Preheat oven to 375°.

Oil 4½″ x 13″, 5″ x 12″, or 5″ x 14″ pan (about 3 inches deep). Line with wax paper. Spread paper lightly with butter and sprinkle with a little flour.

Beat eggs, sugar, and vanilla together at high speed until very light and fluffy (about 10 minutes). Combine cocoa, almonds, and flour in a bowl and beat a few times with a wire whisk. Add to egg mixture, a little at a time, folding in gently with spatula. Slowly add melted butter, folding in gently. Do not over mix. Pour into prepared pan. Bake 20–25 minutes, or until toothpick comes out clean. Cool in pan 5 minutes. Remove from pan and cool completely on a rack.

Frosting: Melt chocolate with milk and coffee in top of double boiler. Remove from heat and stir some of mixture into egg yolks. Add yolk mixture to chocolate, return to heat and stir until thick and shiny (about 2 minutes). Remove from heat and turn into 2-quart bowl. Combine sugar and water in small saucepan and heat to soft ball stage (230°–234°). While syrup is heating, beat egg whites until soft peaks form. Slowly pour hot syrup into egg whites, beating constantly until stiff shiny peaks are formed. Fold into chocolate mixture. Whip cream and gently fold into frosting. Chill overnight.

To assemble: Coat top and sides of cake with frosting. Gently press chocolate shavings into frosting, covering top and sides generously.

PATIO DINNER PARTY

8 people

* Do Ahead
** Freeze

** Party Pork Balls
* Butterflied Leg of Lamb
or
* Barbecued Chicken
* Zucchini and Corn Casserole
* Tomatoes Filled with Spinach
  Soufflé
* Tossed Salad
** Camembert French Bread
* Caramel Custard with Brandy
  Sauce
* Chocolate Chip Cake

This meal is fantastic whether you eat it indoors or out-doors. However, because of the cooking time for the lamb and the chicken, whoever is grilling will have to spend some time with it. Everything else is done ahead. Dishes to be heated will require a minimum of attention.

PARTY PORK BALLS

Can be done ahead and just heated before serving. Combine pork balls and dip in a chafing dish, or place dip dish in center of a tray and surround with pork balls. Add color with minced parsley.

Pork Balls:

1½ pounds ground pork
¾ cup quick or old-fashioned
    oats, uncooked
1 egg, beaten
1 tablespoon grated onion
2 teaspoons salt
½ teaspoon pepper
½ cup milk

Dip:

1 cup pineapple juice
1 tablespoon cornstarch
3 tablespoons brown sugar
¼ teaspoon ginger
1 tablespoon catsup

Pork Balls: Thoroughly combine all ingredients. Shape to form small balls, using one tablespoon of meat mixture for each ball. Fry over low heat in a skillet about 25 minutes, or until cooked through.

Dip: Combine all ingredients in small saucepan. Stir until cornstarch is dissolved. Cook over medium heat, stirring constantly, until sauce comes to a boil and thickens. Continue cooking over low heat until clear, stirring frequently.

BUTTERFLIED LEG OF LAMB

8 servings

What a treat! Save this one for company, since lamb has gotten to be such a luxury. Don't forget the mint jelly. Have the lamb butterflied by making a series of small incisions (like letting out seams) so the lamb will lie flat.

1 leg of lamb (6–7 pounds), boned and butterflied
1 medium onion, chopped fine
3 large cloves garlic, minced
¾ cup olive oil or vegetable oil
½ cup dry white wine
¼ cup chopped parsley
juice of 1 lemon

2 tablespoons Dijon-style mustard
1 teaspoon salt
1 teaspoon basil
1 teaspoon oregano
½ teaspoon each pepper, rosemary, thyme, and marjoram
1 bay leaf, crushed

The day before your party, place lamb in a large plastic bag or shallow pan. Combine remaining ingredients and mix well. Pour marinade over lamb and refrigerate. Turn occasionally so that the marinade penetrates both sides. Remove from refrigerator at least 1 hour before cooking.

To broil on outside grill, turn and baste with marinade frequently for approximately 40 minutes. Test with a sharp knife—the meat should be pink.

To broil indoors, preheat broiler. Place meat, fat side up, in broiler pan. Broil about 4 inches from heat for 10 minutes. Turn, baste with marinade, and broil for another 10 minutes. Turn meat fat side up and baste with marinade. Turn oven temperature to 425° and roast for 15–20 minutes for slightly pink meat.

BARBECUED CHICKEN

8 servings

My father has to be the best chicken cooker anywhere! And the best chicken he does is outside on a grill, either charcoal or gas. He cuts it in halves and marinates it for a day or two. When it has finished cooking, he sometimes cuts it with poultry shears into serving pieces. Chicken stays juicier when cooked in halves.

Marinade:
1½ cups dry white wine
1 tablespoon seasoned salt

½ cup finely chopped onion
2 large cloves garlic, minced

2 large broilers, cut in half

Combine marinade ingredients and stir well. In a large container, place layer of chicken halves, skin side down. Spoon some marinade over them, add more chicken, and spoon remaining marinade on top. Cover with aluminum foil and refrigerate, preferably overnight. Bring to room temperature at least 1 hour before cooking.

Cook on grill about 1 hour and 15 minutes. To test, pierce thickest part of breast with long, sharp fork. Prongs will go in easily if done. The secret to great chicken is to avoid burning. Do not put it on the grill and leave it. You must watch it closely.

ZUCCHINI AND CORN CASSEROLE

8 servings

Every time I serve this dish, someone wants the recipe. It is a wonderful party dish and goes well with any meat, fish, or poultry.

½ stick butter
8 scallions, chopped, including 1 inch of green tops
1½ pounds zucchini, cut in ¼-inch slices
1 16-ounce can kernel corn, drained

1 clove garlic, minced
4 eggs, beaten
1 cup heavy cream
1 cup grated Cheddar cheese
salt and pepper

Preheat oven to 350°.

Melt butter in medium-size saucepan and sauté scallions until soft. Add zucchini. Cover and cook until tender. Do not brown. Mix in corn. Pour vegetable mixture into greased baking dish. Sprinkle garlic on top. Stir cream into eggs. Add half the cheese and season with salt and pepper to taste. Pour into baking dish and sprinkle with remaining cheese. Bake 30 minutes.

TOMATOES FILLED WITH SPINACH SOUFFLÉ

6–12 servings

A great way to look fancy in no time and with little effort.

6 large tomatoes, split in half, or 8 medium tomatoes with tops sliced off
salt and pepper

3 packages frozen spinach soufflé, thawed
grated Parmesan cheese

Scoop out tomatoes. Salt and pepper the insides and fill with spinach. Sprinkle with Parmesan cheese. Tomatoes may be refrigerated at this point. *Preheat oven to 350°.* Bake 15–20 minutes.

CAMEMBERT FRENCH BREAD

8 servings

When you want to "dress up" a meal, think of this yummy bread. It's perfect with soup too.

1 loaf French bread
1 stick butter
4 ounces Camembert cheese, cut into small pieces

1 tablespoon grated onion
½ teaspoon basil
½ teaspoon salt

Preheat oven to 350°.
Slice the bread in half horizontally. In a saucepan, cook butter, cheese, onion, basil, and salt for 5 minutes, stirring to break up the cheese. Spread half the mixture on bottom half of bread. Cover with top half and spread top with remaining cheese mixture. Wrap securely in aluminum foil. Bake for 15 minutes; open foil and bake 5 more minutes. Slice diagonally into 2-inch slices. The bread may be frozen before baking, thawed, and baked as above.

CARAMEL CUSTARD WITH BRANDY SAUCE

8 servings

Very light and refreshing, this is a perfect warm weather dessert. Custard can be topped with whipped cream and chopped nuts in addition to or instead of the Brandy Sauce.

Custard:

- 2 3-ounce packages egg custard mix
- 6 tablespoons sugar
- 2 tablespoons instant coffee powder
- ¼ teaspoon cinnamon
- 3 cups milk
- 1 cup heavy cream
- 1 teaspoon vanilla

Brandy Sauce:

- 1 cup sugar
- ½ cup water
- ¼ cup brandy

Custard: Combine custard mix, sugar, coffee, and cinnamon in a saucepan. Mix well. Blend in milk and cream. Bring quickly to a boil, stirring constantly. Mixture will be thin. Remove from heat and stir in vanilla. Pour into 5-cup ring mold which has been rinsed with cold water and sprayed with vegetable oil. Cool slightly and refrigerate at least 4 hours. Unmold. Serve topped with Brandy Sauce.

Brandy Sauce: Quickly boil sugar and water, stirring constantly until sugar is dissolved. Remove from heat and stir in brandy. Serve the sauce warm or cold.

CHOCOLATE CHIP CAKE

16 servings

So easy and so good. Looks especially nice when baked in a Bundt pan.

1 18½-ounce package
yellow cake mix
4 eggs
½ cup oil
1 cup water
1 teaspoon vanilla
1 3¾-ounce package instant
vanilla pudding

1 4-ounce bar German sweet
chocolate, grated
1 cup chocolate chips
3 tablespoons powdered
sugar

Preheat oven to 350°.

In a large bowl blend first 6 ingredients and mix until smooth. Fold in grated chocolate and chocolate chips. Pour into greased and floured 10-inch Bundt pan. Bake for 50–60 minutes, or until toothpick comes out clean. Set pan on rack for 20 minutes. Turn cake out onto serving dish. Dust top with sifted powdered sugar.

DINNER ITALIANO

■ ■

8 people

* Do Ahead
** Freeze

* **Melon Balls and Prosciutto (Italian Ham)**
* **Breaded Artichoke Hearts**
** **Manicotti with Tomato Sauce**
** **Veal Stuffed Zucchini**
* **Tossed Salad**
** **Garlic Bread**
** **Biscuit Tortoni**

Everyone seems to love Italian food. This meal can be served either as a formal dinner or a buffet. You could also set up two bridge tables and cover them with red and white checkered tablecloths. Use a bottle of Chianti for a centerpiece—your guests will love it. All these recipes are quite easy, and everything is made ahead.

MELON BALLS AND PROSCIUTTO

8 servings

A different way to serve this popular combination. Try using both honeydew and cantaloupe for color and flavor contrast.

1 honeydew or cantaloupe melon (or ½ of each)　　**¼ pound prosciutto**

Cut large melon balls. Cut prosciutto into 1-inch squares. Fold a few times and spear each with toothpick, then spear melon ball. Arrange balls on serving plate with toothpicks straight up, and decorate plate with Italian parsley. Chill.

BREADED ARTICHOKE HEARTS

8 servings

Italian-style seasoned bread crumbs provide a flavorful coating, or you may use herb-flavored crumbs you make yourself by whirling packaged bread stuffing in a blender.

4 4½-ounce jars marinated artichoke hearts, drained　　**1½ cup flavored bread crumbs**

¼ cup grated Romano cheese

Preheat oven to 375°.

Place cheese and bread crumbs in a bag. Add artichoke hearts and shake in bag until well coated. Spread on lightly greased baking sheet and bake for 15 minutes.

MANICOTTI

Tender, light, and absolutely delicious, these filled crêpes (or pancakes) are often the first choice for a special birthday dinner. And they're very easy to prepare. A square electric frying pan makes it even easier. The mozzarella cheese will be easier to grate if you put it in the freezer for 20 minutes.

Crêpes:

1 cup all-purpose flour
1 cup cold water
4 eggs

Filling:

2 pounds ricotta cheese
2 eggs
5 tablespoons grated Romano cheese
3 8-ounce packages mozzarella cheese, grated

Crêpes: *Heat a square electric fry pan to 325°.* Combine all crêpe ingredients and mix well. Grease pan lightly. Cover bottom completely with a thin layer of batter and cook on one side only, for about 3 minutes. Remove and cut into 4 squares. (Or bake 4-inch round crêpes on a griddle.)

Filling: Mix filling ingredients thoroughly. Place on manicotti crêpes and roll into logs. Place logs in a greased baking dish and cover with Tomato Sauce. If you freeze the logs, do not cover with sauce—freeze sauce separately. Pour over logs before baking. *Preheat oven to 350°.* Bake for 1 hour.

TOMATO SAUCE:

Approximately 8 cups

2 28-ounce cans tomatoes
½ cup chopped onion
1 clove garlic, minced
3 tablespoons olive oil
1 8-ounce can tomato sauce
2 6-ounce cans tomato paste

1 cup water
1 teaspoon basil
2 tablespoons parsley
2 teaspoons salt
¼ teaspoon pepper

Puree tomatoes in blender or food processor. Sauté onion and garlic in oil. Add tomatoes and all remaining ingredients. Simmer over low heat 1 hour.

VEAL STUFFED ZUCCHINI

This dish can also be served plain, but I prefer it with the Tomato Sauce.

4 large zucchini, 1–1½
  pounds each
6 tablespoons olive oil
1 cup chopped onion
2 cloves garlic, minced
½ pound ground veal
½ pound ground pork
1 cup bread crumbs
2 egg yolks

4 tablespoons chopped
  parsley
6 tablespoons chopped fresh
  dill or 2 tablespoons
  dried dill weed
  salt and pepper
4 tablespoons freshly grated
  Parmesan cheese

Preheat oven to 350°.

Cut zucchini in half lengthwise. Scoop out pulp, leaving a firm shell. Reserve 2 cups chopped pulp. Heat 3 tablespoons of the oil and sauté onion and garlic until onion is wilted. Add meat and cook until it loses its pink color. Add reserved pulp and cook for 3 minutes. Add half the bread crumbs, the egg yolks, parsley, and dill. Remove from heat and mix well. Salt and pepper insides of zucchini. Stuff zucchini with meat mixture. Top with Parmesan cheese, remaining bread crumbs and 6 tablespoons olive oil. Bake 30 minutes. Can be frozen, thawed, and then baked.

GARLIC BREAD

Perfect for an Italian dinner, and an excellent standby for any meal.

1 large long loaf Italian
  bread
1 stick butter, softened

1 4-ounce jar garlic spread
  concentrate
  oregano

Preheat oven to 375°.

Cut bread into ½-inch slices, leaving them attached at bottom. Combine butter and garlic spread and mix well. Spread on both sides of each slice, and along the entire top of loaf. Place loaf on aluminum foil. Sprinkle oregano on top. Wrap loaf securely in foil. Bake 15–20 minutes; open foil and cook 5 minutes more. May be frozen and thawed before baking.

BISCUIT TORTONI

12 servings

These are nothing like what you have ever bought. They are extremely light and delicious. Cook in advance and freeze. You might want to use a fancy 1-quart mold instead of individual cups. You will need a candy thermometer and 2½-inch paper muffin liners.

¼ cup water
¾ cup sugar
3 egg whites, at room
  temperature
  dash of salt
¼ cup whole blanched
  almonds

1¾ teaspoons almond extract
1½ cups heavy cream
¾ teaspoon vanilla
12 maraschino or candied
  cherries

Mix the water with the sugar in a 1-quart saucepan and stir over low heat to dissolve. Boil uncovered, without stirring, to 236° on candy thermometer. Beat egg whites with salt just until stiff peaks form. Pour hot syrup in thin stream over whites, beating constantly until very stiff peaks form when beater is raised. Cover and refrigerate for 30 minutes.

Preheat oven to 350°. Place blanched almonds in shallow baking pan and bake for 10 minutes. Chop almonds fine or grind fine in blender or food processor. Turn into small bowl and stir in 1½ teaspoons of the almond extract. Set aside. Whip cream with ¼ teaspoon almond extract and the vanilla, until quite stiff. With rubber scraper gently fold cream into egg whites until well combined. Line muffin pan with 12 paper liners. Spoon mixture into paper liners. Sprinkle with ground almonds and top each with a cherry. Cover with foil and freeze overnight or for at least 4 hours.

For longer storage, remove from pan and wrap well. Will keep 1 month. If you use one mold instead of individual muffin liners, freeze until firm enough to unmold. To unmold, run a small spatula around the edge of mold and dip quickly into hot water. Invert onto serving dish. Sprinkle with almond mixture. Return to freezer until ready to serve. Decorate with whipped cream and cherries.

ALL-DONE-AHEAD
DINNER PARTY

■■■■■■■■■■■■■■■■■■■■■■■■■■■■

8–10 people

* Do Ahead
** Freeze

* **Shrimp Mold**
* **Crab and Cheese Melt-aways**
* **Rolled Chicken Cutlets with
Cheese Sauce**
or
* **Chicken Breasts with Three
Soups and Rice**
* **Lemon Salad Mold**
* **Spinach Salad**
** **Rolls**
* **Chocolate Mousse Angel
Food Cake**

Every one wants a few really easy to prepare chicken recipes for last-minute entertaining, serving a lot of people easily, when too busy to cook, or just because they are so good. The chicken is as tender and juicy as can be, and if your casserole has to sit awhile before serving, it will still be moist and flavorful. These recipes are also suitable for reheating. You will find this meal needs very little of your attention after the party has begun. Unmold Lemon Salad Mold onto serving platter and refrigerate before guests arrive. Split, butter, and wrap the rolls in aluminum foil in advance and then heat. The refrigerated Chocolate Mousse Angel Food Cake can be made the day before or the morning of your dinner party.

SHRIMP MOLD

16–20 servings

This dish is especially attractive in a fish mold. Decorate with ripe olives and parsley, and serve with crackers. Can be made a day or two in advance. Also good as a salad mold with a meal.

1 10¾-ounce can tomato soup, undiluted
1 8-ounce package cream cheese, at room temperature
1½ envelopes unflavored gelatin

½ cup cold water
1 cup mayonnaise
1½ cups finely chopped celery
½ cup finely chopped onion
1 pound shrimp, cooked, cleaned, and diced

Bring soup to a boil, being careful that it does not burn. Add cream cheese and stir until melted. Dissolve gelatin in cold water. Add to hot mixture. Add all other ingredients. Pour into a 6-cup mold which has been rinsed with cold water and sprayed with vegetable oil. Refrigerate.

CRAB AND CHEESE MELT-AWAYS

40 appetizers

These little appetizers will garner raves for the cook. Make them ahead and place on a cookie sheet. Just stick them under the broiler at the last minute. Can be frozen if you use fresh or canned crab.

1 stick butter, softened
4 ounces pasteurized process Cheddar cheese spread, at room temperature

1 cup shredded crab meat
12 miniature or party tea rolls

Blend butter and cheese thoroughly, preferably in a food processor. Combine with crab meat. Split rolls and spread each side with mixture. Place under broiler until bubbly and light brown.

ROLLED CHICKEN CUTLETS WITH CHEESE SAUCE

10 servings

Surprisingly easy and delicious. This recipe can be increased for a large group and does not take long to bake. Bake in a shallow oven-to-table casserole. It's an attractive dish for either a buffet or a sit-down dinner. Serve with rice.

5 whole chicken breasts,
   skinned, boned, and halved
   mayonnaise
   crushed cornflakes

Cheese Sauce:

½ cup mayonnaise
½ cup milk
½ cup grated Cheddar
   cheese
1 teaspoon thyme
   minced parsley

Preheat oven to 350°.

Spread chicken breasts on both sides with mayonnaise. Dip one side into crushed cornflakes and roll, coated side out, securing with toothpick. Place in buttered baking dish so they do not touch. Bake 35 minutes. Remove toothpicks.

Sauce: In saucepan, combine mayonnaise, milk, cheese, and thyme. Heat until bubbly.

Serve over chicken rolls. Decorate with parsley.

CHICKEN BREASTS WITH THREE SOUPS AND RICE

10 servings

This recipe was once increased to serve 125 ladies at a luncheon. It is easy to make and is always a great hit. You may increase the number of servings by adding a couple of chicken breasts to the recipe.

1 6-ounce package long-grain and wild rice mix
1 stick butter, melted
5 whole chicken breasts, skinned, boned, and halved
1 10¾-ounce can cream of chicken soup, undiluted
1 10¾-ounce can cream of mushroom soup, undiluted

1 10¾-ounce can cream of celery soup, undiluted
½ cup sherry
1 teaspoon thyme
1 cup grated sharp Cheddar cheese
1 cup thinly sliced almonds

Preheat oven to 350°.
Sprinkle rice in 13″ x 9″ oven-proof dish. Spread package of seasonings over rice. Pour melted butter over seasonings. Roll up each chicken half, secure with toothpick, and place on rice. Combine the three soups, sherry, and thyme and pour over chicken. Sprinkle with cheese and top with almonds. Bake uncovered for 2 hours.

LEMON SALAD MOLD

8–10 servings

Delicious and light. Serve on curly lettuce.

1 6-ounce package lemon gelatin
1¾ cups boiling water
10 ice cubes
1 6-ounce can frozen lemonade concentrate

1 cup heavy cream, whipped
4 cups of 2 fruits such as bananas, seedless grapes, mandarin oranges, or pineapple

Dissolve gelatin in boiling water. Add ice cubes quickly and stir until melted. Add frozen lemonade and stir. Refrigerate until almost set. Add whipped cream and fruit and combine gently. Pour into 12-cup ring mold which has been rinsed with cold water and sprayed with vegetable oil. Refrigerate.

SPINACH SALAD

8–10 servings

A colorful favorite.

2 pounds fresh spinach
1 medium-size red onion, sliced
½ cup vegetable oil
4 tablespoons wine vinegar
2 tablespoons lemon juice
1 teaspoon sugar
1 teaspoon salt

freshly ground pepper
1 12-ounce or 1-pound box mushrooms, sliced
2 hard-cooked eggs, chopped coarse
8 slices cooked bacon, crumbled

Wash spinach well, pat dry, and tear into bite-size pieces. Place in large plastic bag with onion slices and chill. Several hours before serving, combine oil, vinegar, lemon juice, sugar, salt, and pepper and pour over mushrooms in small bowl. Allow to marinate in refrigerator. When ready to serve, pour mushrooms and dressing over salad greens, add eggs and bacon, and toss gently.

CHOCOLATE MOUSSE ANGEL FOOD CAKE

10 servings

Angel food cake is a treat in any form, and adding chocolate mousse makes it that much better. Make it well ahead—it should be refrigerated 6–24 hours before serving.

1 18½-ounce package angel food cake mix
2 4-ounce bars German sweet chocolate

6 tablespoons water
2 teaspoons vanilla
2 cups heavy cream, whipped

Bake cake according to directions on package. Cool cake in pan on a rack for 1 hour, remove from pan, and slice with a serrated knife to make two layers. Melt chocolate with water. Beat until smooth and add vanilla. Cool to room temperature. Fold into whipped cream. Place bottom layer on serving platter and spread with some of the mousse. Add top layer and cover top and sides with remaining mousse. Refrigerate.

LARGE PARTIES
FOR
SPECIAL
OCCASIONS

■ Sometimes it takes a holiday or other special occasion to give us the perfect excuse for a large party. It also supplies a theme to build the party around. Use your imagination—the possibilities are endless. It isn't necessary to go all-out on decorations or food, but a theme will give your party focus and add much to its enjoyment. For instance, your invitation for a party around Valentine's Day may make no mention of the holiday, but you could serve your dessert in a heart-shaped mold and choose pink carnations for a centerpiece.

■ The recipes in this section can easily be doubled, tripled, or further increased for a large party and have been selected with that in mind. If you are cooking for a large crowd, prepare the food in stages. For example, if the entree calls for cooked chicken, cook, bone, and refrigerate it, then complete the preparation on the following day.

To make your large party a success, keep in mind the following suggestions:

■ Think of the size of your oven when planning your menu. Go for one dish to be heated if you have one oven, or include a dish that can be heated on top of the stove, and add more cold foods.

■ Make it easier on yourself with a lot of easy-to-prepare recipes.

■ Use your freezer for storing dishes that can be made well in advance.

■ Borrow refrigerator space, if necessary. Check with friends and neighbors ahead of time.

■ Make the foods which can be frozen first, then any dips, spreads, or molds, and finally the cold hors d'oeuvres.

■ Have all the trays and serving dishes polished and ready for food. You don't want to be digging into cabinets at the last minute. Also, check your chafing dishes to make sure the burners can light.

■ Rent, buy, or borrow loads of glasses—more than the number of people you are having. The same goes for cocktail napkins.

■ Have plenty of ashtrays around. You would be amazed what some of your best friends do with cigarettes and ashes at a crowded party.

■ If you are big on guests and small on space, clear out as much furniture as possible. Tables and chairs are usually the first things to go.

■ Have a place set aside for coats and boots. Rent portable coat racks if necessary.

AFTER THE FOOTBALL GAME BUFFET DINNER

16 people

* Do Ahead
* * Freeze

> * Kir, or Chablis Cassis
> * Pea Soup and Crab Mold
> * Steak Tartare
> * * Chicken Casserole with
>   Sausages and Mushrooms
> * Combination Rice Casserole
> * Orange Sherbet Salad
> * Cranberry and Raspberry
>   Cream Mold
> * Tossed Salad
> * Rolls
> * Crêpes Filled with
>   Chocolate Mousse

Your guests will be very hungry after spending the afternoon out of doors. The hors d'oeuvres are light but plentiful,
and the Kir is a perfect start to a substantial meal. Your
buffet table will look complete with a hollowed pumpkin
filled with fresh brown and yellow chrysanthemums set on
a bed of colored leaves. Tie your napkins with a thick fall-
color yarn.

KIR, OR CHABLIS CASSIS

6 servings

A wonderful French aperitif to substitute for the before-dinner cocktail. Serve with or without ice cubes in a wine glass. A bottle of Chablis will provide six ½-cup servings. Triple the recipe for sixteen people.

1 fifth Chablis
½ cup crème de cassis
  (black currant liqueur)
6 strips of lemon peel

Remove approximately ½ cup of Chablis from the bottle and pour in crème de cassis. Replace the cork partially and shake the bottle gently. Refrigerate. A small strip of lemon peel can be added to each glass.

PEA SOUP AND CRAB MOLD

16–20 servings

A very special elegant touch for any occasion. Use a ring- or fish-shaped 1-quart mold. Do not use a tin mold, as it may affect the flavor of the crab meat. Make this a day or two ahead. Serve with a hard pumpernickel flat bread or water crackers. Decorate with parsley. This refreshing mold is also a real favorite as an entree for a luncheon. Use frozen king crab or canned snow crab.

2 envelopes unflavored
  gelatin
2 cups water, including
  liquid from crab meat
1 2⅞-ounce package green
  pea soup mix
½ 10-ounce package frozen
  green peas
1 teaspoon dry mustard

3 dashes Tabasco
2 tablespoons lemon juice
1½ 8-ounce packages cream
  cheese
2 cups sour cream
1 12-ounce package frozen
  crab meat, thawed, or
  2 6-ounce cans crab meat,
  flaked

In a saucepan, sprinkle gelatin over water and crab meat liquid. Add soup mix and green peas, cover, and bring to a boil. Transfer to a blender or food processor. Add mustard, Tabasco, lemon juice, and cream cheese. spin until smooth. Transfer to a large bowl and stir in sour cream with a wire whisk. Add crab meat. Pour into a mold which has been rinsed with cold water and sprayed with vegetable oil. Refrigerate. Loosen mold by running a grapefruit knife around the edges. Invert on serving tray.

STEAK TARTARE

8 servings

Those who like this really love it! Buy meat the day of your party. Serve on a platter with plenty of parsley, onion rings, capers and hard pumpernickel bread. You may wish to roll meat in 1½-inch balls. The condiments may be served in small bowls around the platter. After mixing, refrigerate at least two hours before serving. Double the recipe for sixteen people.

1¼ pounds very lean chopped
    sirloin or tenderloin
½ cup finely chopped onions
1 egg
1 tablespoon capers
1 teaspoon chives
1 teaspoon minced parsley
1 teaspoon Dijon-style
    mustard

¾ teaspoon salt
½ teaspoon freshly ground
    pepper
1 tablespoon Worcestershire
    sauce
2 tablespoons olive oil
¼ teaspoon Tabasco
1 tablespoon steak sauce
1 tablespoon Cognac

Combine all ingredients and refrigerate. Mound in center of platter. Garnish with a sprinkling of additional parsley.

CHICKEN CASSEROLE WITH SAUSAGES AND MUSHROOMS

8 servings

This very popular savory casserole is a perennial favorite. Preparation takes a little time, but it's very easy to make. You can cut the time down by substituting precooked sausage links cut into ½-inch slices and browned for the sausage balls. The casserole can be prepared a few days in advance. Freezes well. Double the recipe for sixteen people.

½ pound bulk pork sausage
½ pound mushrooms, sliced
2 tablespoons butter
4 whole chicken breasts,
    cooked, boned, and cut
    into 2-inch chunks

Cream Sauce:
½ stick butter
¼ cup all-purpose flour
    salt and pepper to taste
2 cups chicken stock
2/3 cup heavy cream

Topping:
½ 8-ounce bag herb-seasoned
    stuffing
½ stick butter, melted

Roll the pork sausage into tiny balls, brown well, and drain on paper towels. Sauté the mushrooms in the butter and drain.

Preheat oven to 350°. In a 13" x 9" casserole, layer chicken, sausage, and mushrooms, in that order. Top with cream sauce. Spread topping evenly over all. Bake for 45 minutes, or until heated through.

Cream Sauce: Melt butter in saucepan and stir in flour, salt, and pepper. Slowly add chicken stock and cream. Heat, stirring constantly, until thick.

Topping: Combine stuffing with melted butter.

COMBINATION RICE CASSEROLE

8 servings

This is good with so many dishes. It can be baked before your guests arrive. Keep it covered with a few towels—it will stay warm for hours. The nuts float to the top in cooking and the casserole looks very attractive. Double the recipe for sixteen people.

3 tablespoons butter
1 medium onion, chopped
1 cup long-grain rice
½ cup wild rice, washed with cold water and drained

½ cup thinly sliced almonds
3¼ cups chicken stock
chopped parsley

Preheat oven to 375°.

Heat butter in a skillet and sauté onion and white and wild rice for 5 minutes. Add nuts and stir. Transfer to a 2-quart casserole. Add the chicken stock and stir. Cover and bake for 45 minutes, or until rice is tender and liquid is absorbed. Garnish with parsley.

ORANGE SHERBET SALAD

10 servings

This mold is as pretty to look at as it is good to eat. This size mold will be sufficient for sixteen people if you are serving another salad with it.

1 6-ounce package orange
 gelatin
1 cup boiling water
1 pint orange sherbet
1 11-ounce can mandarin
 oranges, drained

1 10-ounce can crushed
 pineapple
1 cup heavy cream, whipped

Dissolve gelatin in boiling water. Add sherbet and stir well. Add oranges and pineapple and fold in whipped cream. Pour into a 2-quart mold which has been rinsed with cold water and sprayed with vegetable oil. Refrigerate. To serve, unmold on a serving platter. Deep green spinach leaves would make an attractive garnish.

CRANBERRY AND RASPBERRY CREAM MOLD

10 servings

A richly colored concoction suitable for any occasion. This size mold will be sufficient for sixteen people if you are serving another salad with it.

1 3-ounce package
 raspberry gelatin
1¼ cups boiling water
1 8-ounce package cream
 cheese

1 14-ounce jar cranberry-
 orange relish
1 cup miniature
 marshmallows
½ cup chopped walnuts

Dissolve gelatin in water. Blend cream cheese and relish into gelatin mixture. Add marshmallows and nuts. Pour into a 6-cup mold which has been rinsed with cold water and sprayed with vegetable oil. Yellow and pale green leaves of escarole would make an attractive garnish.

CRÊPES FILLED WITH CHOCOLATE MOUSSE

Approximately 34 crêpes

These are heavenly. Very rich and a perfect way to end a meal. Plan to serve 1–1½ crêpes per person. Crêpes (unfilled) freeze well.

Crêpes:
- 4 eggs
- ¼ teaspoon salt
- 2 cups all-purpose flour
- 2¼ cups milk
- 1 stick butter, melted

Topping:
- 1½ cups heavy cream
- ¼ cup powdered sugar
- ½ teaspoon vanilla
- ½ cup toasted thinly sliced almonds

Chocolate Mousse:
- 8 eggs
- 1 12-ounce package chocolate bits
- 4 tablespoons rum
- 2 teaspoons powdered instant coffee
- 1 cup sugar

Crêpes: In a mixing bowl, combine eggs and salt. Gradually add flour alternately with milk, beating with electric mixer or whisk until smooth. Beat in melted butter. (Or combine all crêpe ingredients in a blender or food processor and blend until smooth.) Refrigerate batter at least 1 hour. In a lightly greased crêpe pan over medium-high heat, pour 2 to 3 tablespoons batter. Turn crêpe when lightly browned and cook about 30 seconds on other side. Cool crêpes in a single layer on absorbent paper. To freeze, it is best to put a square of wax paper between each crêpe and place them in freezer bags. Make sure they are thoroughly defrosted before taking apart to fill.

Mousse: Separate eggs, placing egg yolks in a bowl, four whites in a second bowl, and remaining four whites in a third bowl. Melt chocolate over low heat. Add yolks, one at a time, beating well after each addition. Blend in rum and coffee. Remove from heat and cool slightly. Beat 4 egg whites in each bowl until frothy (beating all 8 together will not give you enough volume), gradually adding ½ cup sugar to each bowl. Beat until stiff peaks form. Stir small amount of whites into chocolate mixture. Combine whites and fold chocolate mixture into them.

Topping: Whip cream. Fold in powdered sugar and vanilla.

Crêpes can be filled two hours before and refrigerated. Or fill just before serving. It will take only a few minutes. Top each with a dollop of whipped cream and a few sliced almonds.

SPRING LUNCHEON

18 people

* Do Ahead
** Freeze

* **May Wine Punch**
* **Red Hot Chicken Wings**
** **Spaghetti Primavera**
* **Dilled Tomatoes**
** **French Mustard Bread**
* **Strawberry Meringue Tartlets**

Everyone is just starting to see signs of spring, and either a committee luncheon is scheduled or you just want to have a lovely gathering for your friends. This is a delightful meal in early spring when feathery dill and fresh strawberries appear in the markets. The easy May Wine Punch is a cinch to make. A big bunch of daisies will look terrific arranged in a basket with a few colorful anemones or tulips for your centerpiece.

MAY WINE PUNCH

24 cups

A very good and easy punch. Serve in a pitcher or punch bowl.

1 gallon red jug-wine, chilled

2 quarts ginger ale, chilled

2 quarts fresh strawberries, washed

Do not cut or remove stems of strawberries. Combine all ingredients and serve.

RED HOT CHICKEN WINGS

30 pieces

My nephew in Colorado says these are the rage out there. They are very easy to prepare and really "red hot." You may wish to adjust the hot sauce to taste.

15 chicken wings

2 tablespoons bottled hot sauce

½ stick butter

¾ cup bottled blue cheese dressing

Preheat broiler.

Cut each wing into thirds. Discard tips. Broil chicken wings for 5 minutes, turn and broil another 5 minutes. Watch carefully so they do not burn. In a saucepan, combine hot sauce and butter and heat until butter is melted. In a large pan, place a batch of wings and some of the sauce. Shake the pan to coat the wings. Serve with a dish of blue cheese dressing as a dip. After coating, you may refrigerate and reheat in preheated 350° oven for 10 minutes, or until hot.

SPAGHETTI PRIMAVERA

18 servings

This is a very popular dish any time of the year. Spaghetti Primavera is usually prepared at the last minute, but this version can be done well ahead.

1 bunch broccoli, trimmed and cut into flowerets
1 10-ounce package frozen asparagus spears, thawed
1 9-ounce package frozen Italian green beans, thawed
1 10-ounce package frozen green peas, thawed
¼ cup olive oil
3 large cloves garlic, chopped fine
4 cups ham (1 pound), julienned
12 ounces mushrooms, sliced

½ cup finely chopped parsley
¾ teaspoon crushed red pepper
2 16-ounce packages thin spaghetti or linguine
½ cup butter
½ cup all-purpose flour
2 teaspoons salt
¼ teaspoon freshly ground pepper
5 cups milk
1½ cups freshly grated Parmesan cheese

In medium-size saucepan, cook broccoli in boiling water to cover for 3 minutes. Drain and cool immediately in a large pan of ice water. Drain. Cut asparagus spears into 4 pieces. In a large bowl, combine broccoli, asparagus, beans, and peas and reserve. In a large skillet, heat oil. Add garlic, ham, mushrooms, parsley, and red pepper. Sauté, stirring, for 3 minutes. Add reserved vegetables and heat through. In a large pan, cook spaghetti according to package directions. Drain well and keep warm. In same large pan, melt butter over low heat and blend in flour, salt, and pepper to form a smooth paste. Gradually stir in milk and, stirring constantly, cook about 10 minutes, or until thickened and smooth. Add Parmesan and cook, stirring, until smooth. Add spaghetti and vegetable mixture; toss quickly to blend. Serve immediately or place in two greased 13" x 9" baking dishes. Cover tightly and refrigerate up to 2 days. To serve, *preheat oven to 350°*. Bake covered for 45 minutes, or until heated through. Serve with freshly ground pepper.

DILLED TOMATOES

10 servings

A lively addition to a luncheon table. Double the recipe for eighteen people.

1 quart cherry tomatoes	½ teaspoon salt
½ 16-ounce can white onions, drained	½ teaspoon dry mustard
	¼ cup salad oil or olive oil
¼ cup minced fresh dill or 1 tablespoon dried dill weed	2 tablespoons vinegar
	½ teaspoon grated lemon peel

Dip tomatoes in boiling water quickly and remove skins. In a large bowl, combine onions and tomatoes. In a small bowl, combine dill, salt, mustard, oil, and vinegar and blend well. Pour over tomatoes. Sprinkle lemon peel over top. Refrigerate a few hours before serving.

FRENCH MUSTARD BREAD

8–10 servings

Tastes wonderful and freezes well. Double the recipe for eighteen people.

1 stick butter, softened	1 tablespoon sesame seed, toasted
¼ cup minced parsley	
2 tablespoons chopped scallions, including green tops	1 teaspoon lemon juice
	1 large loaf French bread, sliced 1 inch thick
2 tablespoons mustard, preferably Dijon-style	

Preheat oven to 350°.

Thoroughly blend butter, parsley, scallions, mustard, sesame seed, and lemon juice. Spread lightly on both sides of bread. Arrange in single layer on cookie sheets and bake for 20 minutes, or until crisp.

STRAWBERRY MERINGUE TARTLETS

Approximately 32 tartlets

Spectacular and different. Make meringues a day or so ahead. The day of your party, make whipped cream mixture, cover and refrigerate. Wash and hull strawberries. When ready to serve, it will only take you a few minutes to spoon some mixture into meringues and top each with a strawberry. Do not be afraid of the last-minute work—it isn't much.

Meringues:

2 egg whites, at room temperature
¼ teaspoon cream of tartar or ½ teaspoon white vinegar
pinch of salt
½ teaspoon vanilla
½ cup sugar (preferably superfine)

Filling:

1 cup heavy cream
1½ tablespoons powdered sugar
⅓ cup finely chopped toasted almonds
1 teaspoon sherry
2 teaspoons chopped crystallized ginger

Garnish:

32 small strawberries

Meringues: *Preheat oven to 275°.* Combine egg whites, cream of tartar, salt, and vanilla in a bowl. Beat until whites hold soft peaks. Gradually add sugar, a tablespoon at a time, and beat until meringue is very stiff. Cover a cookie sheet with a piece of heavy brown paper. Drop meringue by heaping teaspoonfuls onto paper, using spoon to make a nest in the center. Bake for 1 hour. If they are not dry, return to oven for another 15 minutes or so. When cool, peel from paper.

Filling: Whip cream and sweeten with powdered sugar. Add almonds, sherry and ginger. Refrigerate.

To serve, fill meringue shells with whipped cream mixture. Place a strawberry, tip up, in the center of each.

MIDSUMMER BUFFET

* Do Ahead
** Freeze

* **Planters Punch**
* **Pecan Cheese Ball**
* **Smoked Salmon Soufflé**
* **Cold Fillet of Beef with**
  Sour Cream
* **Spaghetti Salad**
* **Marinated Blanched Vegetables**
  Bread Sticks
* **Angel Food Cake with**
  Strawberry Cream
** **Triple Chocolate Cake**

It's delicious, it's different, it's elegant and it's all cold—which means, of course, no excuses for being in the kitchen. You are in the midst of a hot spell and you have invited a fair number of people to dinner. With this menu, you won't even have to light your stove on the day of your party. Your guests will think you are terrific for coping with all this food in such hot weather. Since this is a buffet, the number of servings each dish will yield will vary with the appetites of your guests. The servings indicated here are average. Put both mouth-watering cakes out and let guests cut their own; usually a small piece of each goes on each plate, for both look too good to resist.

PLANTERS PUNCH

A delicious rum drink. Use frosted tall glasses for this summer drink.

1 Serving	4 Servings
crushed ice	crushed ice
1 jigger orange juice	¾ cup orange juice
2 jiggers pineapple juice	1½ cups pineapple juice
1 jigger water	¾ cup water
1 tablespoon sugar	4 tablespoons sugar
1 jigger light rum	¾ cup light rum
1 jigger dark rum	¾ cup dark rum
1 orange slice	4 orange slices

Mix first 6 ingredients together. Pour dark rum on top. Garnish with an orange slice.

PECAN CHEESE BALL

15–20 servings

Easy. Keeps several weeks under refrigeration. Make two for twenty people.

1 8-ounce package cream cheese, at room temperature
5 ounces Cheddar cheese spread, at room temperature
10 ounces blue cheese, at room temperature

1 small onion, minced
1 clove garlic, minced
2 tablespoons brandy or sherry
½ cup chopped pecans

Beat cheeses until well mixed and fluffy. Add onion, garlic, and brandy. Mix well. Chill. Shape into ball, coating with nuts. Chill again. Serve with crackers.

SMOKED SALMON SOUFFLÉ

Deluxe company dish. Can be prepared up to three days before serving. Do not double since you have plenty of hors d'oeuvres.

1¼ cups finely chopped
onions

2 tablespoons butter

1 pound smoked salmon

2 8-ounce packages cream
cheese, at room
temperature

2 tablespoons finely
chopped dill

1 cup heavy cream

1 10-ounce square loaf
dark bread
parsley

Prepare a 2-cup soufflé dish: cut a length of wax paper long enough to go around dish and fold it in half lengthwise. Wrap around dish and secure with string. Collar should extend 4–5 inches above rim. Sauté onions in butter in a large skillet, stirring occasionally, for 5 minutes. Cool. Remove and discard any bones, skin, or tough parts from the salmon. Chop salmon fine, then put in a large bowl. Add cream cheese and mix well with an electric mixer or by hand. Add onions and dill and blend thoroughly. Mixture should be pale pink and very soft. Beat cream until stiff. Fold into salmon mixture. Spoon mixture into prepared dish. Refrigerate overnight. To serve, remove collar and decorate top with a few sprigs of parsley. Cut bread into triangles and serve beside soufflé.

COLD FILLET OF BEEF
WITH SOUR CREAM

6 servings

Quite easy to prepare and heavenly to taste. The fillet may be served whole with the filling on the side. For twenty people, buy four tenderloin tails, but you'll only have to double the filling recipe.

4 tablespoons butter
1 carrot, chopped
1 stalk celery, chopped
1 bunch scallions or 1
   medium onion, chopped
1 2-pound fillet of beef
   (tail end)
   salt and pepper

Filling:
½ pound slab bacon, cut into
   ¼-inch cubes
1 tablespoon oil
1 clove garlic, minced
1 cup sour cream
1 tablespoon grated onion
1 tablespoon chopped chives
   salt and pepper to taste
   watercress
   cherry tomatoes

Preheat oven to 500°.

In a small roasting pan, heat 2 tablespoons of the butter and sauté carrot, celery, and scallions for 10 minutes. Add the beef, sprinkle with salt and pepper, and dot with remaining 2 tablespoons butter. Roast for 20–25 minutes for rare meat. Let it cool in the pan for 1 hour. Transfer fillet to a serving platter, strain and reserve 1½ tablespoons pan juices for the filling.

Filling: Sauté bacon in oil with garlic until bacon is crisp. Remove the bacon bits with a slotted spoon, drain them on paper towels, and discard the fat. In a bowl, combine sour cream and 1½ tablespoons reserved pan juices with onion and chives. Add bacon bits, salt, and pepper and mix well.

With a sharp knife, cut a wedge along the length of the top of the fillet 1½-inches wide and 1-inch deep and remove it. Fill the cavity with as much filling as it will hold, and pour the remainder into a serving dish. Cut the wedge crosswise into ¾-inch slices; reassemble the wedge and set it on top of the filling. Garnish the fillet with watercress and cherry tomatoes. To serve, cut through the sliced top wedge using the ¾-inch slices as markers to cut all the way through at ¾-inch intervals. The fillet can be prepared the day before, cut and assembled a few hours before serving, then chilled until ready to serve.

SPAGHETTI SALAD

Different and tasty. Prepare and refrigerate a few days in advance. Either chop eggs and mix in or quarter eggs and use to garnish top of salad. Recipe may be doubled or tripled.

8 ounces spaghetti
1 cucumber, chopped
1 bunch radishes, sliced
1 bunch scallions, including
  1 inch of green tops,
  sliced
1 teaspoon salt
½ teaspoon sugar
½ teaspoon pepper
½ teaspoon celery salt
⅛ teaspoon oregano
2 hard-cooked eggs

Dressing:
  1 cup mayonnaise
  ¼ cup sour cream
  ¼ cup milk or
    half-and-half
  ¼ cup bottled cole slaw
    dressing
  1 teaspoon Dijon-style
    mustard

Break spaghetti into quarters. Cook according to package directions in water containing 1 tablespoon oil. Drain. Add remaining ingredients. Dressing: Combine dressing ingredients. Toss dressing and spaghetti mixture. Cover and refrigerate overnight.

MARINATED BLANCHED VEGETABLES

Group the vegetables in big piles on a silver tray. The presentation is very impressive. Use whatever vegetables are plentiful and in season. Think in terms of contrasting colors and different shapes.

1 bag carrots, cut onto ½″ x 3″ sticks

1 bunch broccoli, cut into flowerets

15 stalks asparagus, ends trimmed

1 zucchini, sliced into 1-inch rounds

1 summer squash, sliced into 1-inch rounds tomatoes, cauliflower, green beans, or artichoke hearts

Vinaigrette Dressing:

1¼ cups salad oil

½ cup cider vinegar

4 tablespoons sweet pickle relish

3 tablespoons chopped parsley

1 teaspoon salt

1¼ teaspoons sugar

Blanch all vegetables separately by plunging into boiling water until partially cooked. Immerse in ice water to stop cooking and retain color. Drain and put into separate plastic bags with enough Vinaigrette Dressing to coat. Refrigerate overnight. Drain and arrange in contrasting groups on a tray. Serve cold or at room temperature.

Vinaigrette Dressing: Combine all ingredients in blender for 1 minute. Keeps in refrigerator for weeks.

ANGEL FOOD CAKE WITH STRAWBERRY CREAM

12 servings

Light, wonderful, and lovely. Can be easily assembled and refrigerated a few hours before serving. This will be enough for twenty people if you are serving another dessert with it. Otherwise, make two cakes.

1 14½-ounce package angel food cake mix

2 10-ounce packages frozen sliced strawberries, thawed

1 pint strawberries, hulled

2 cups heavy cream

Bake cake according to package directions. When cool, carefully slice into 3 layers. Drain the thawed strawberries, reserving juice. Reserve 9 fresh strawberries for garnish and slice the rest. Whip the cream. Fold sliced fresh strawberries and the drained strawberries into the whipped cream. Slowly fold in some of the reserved juice, but not enough to make the mixture runny. On a serving platter, spread mixture between layers and on top of cake. Garnish platter around the base of the cake with 6 of the whole strawberries and place the remaining 3 around the top of the cake. Carefully cover with plastic wrap and refrigerate until ready to serve.

TRIPLE CHOCOLATE CAKE

12 servings

A wonderful moist and rich cake. Recipe can be doubled.

cocoa
1 18½-ounce package deep chocolate or devil's food cake mix
1 4-ounce package instant chocolate pudding
¾ cup sour cream
½ cup vegetable oil
½ cup water
½ cup toasted chopped almonds

¼ cup mayonnaise
4 eggs
3 tablespoons almond liqueur
1 teaspoon almond extract
1 cup chocolate chips

Glaze:

1 cup powdered sugar
3 tablespoons milk
1 teaspoon almond extract

Preheat oven to 350°.

Grease 10-inch Bundt pan and dust with cocoa. Place next 10 ingredients in a large bowl and beat 2 minutes at medium speed. Mix in chocolate chips. Pour into pan. Bake 50–55 minutes, or until toothpick comes out clean. Cool on rack 10 minutes before removing from pan. Place warm cake on serving dish and drizzle with glaze.

Glaze: Mix all ingredients thoroughly in small bowl. Let stand at room temperature until ready to glaze cake.

SUPER BOWL
DAY BUFFET DINNER

* Do Ahead
** Freeze

* **Keg of Beer**
* **Smoked Salmon and Boursin in Cucumber Cups**
* **Stuffed French Bread**
* **Sweet Brie and Crackers**
* **Bourbon Hot Dogs**
* **Chicken, Shrimp, and Artichoke Casserole**
* **Slow Cooker Pilaf**
* **Strawberry and Banana Mold**
* **Tossed Green Salad**
* **Herbed Monkey Bread**
** **Cheese Cake Squares**
* **Praline Strips**

Arrange a betting pool for your guests for the big game. Call an avid football fan who will be pleased to set up and run the betting. TV sets should be placed in different rooms—serious viewers will want to concentrate on the game. The hors d'oeuvres will not require your time in the kitchen at the last minute so you are free to join your guests. Make a pom-pom or two for either side of your flower arrangement for that extra special touch. The occasion is perfect for a keg of beer. If a few guests prefer a drink from the bar, tell them where the liquor is and to please help themselves.

KEG OF BEER

Great for a large group of guests. If you can round up lots of beer mugs, terrific. If not, buy the large plastic-coated disposable beer containers. The liquor store near you will provide and set up the necessary tap, ice, tub, and instructions. They will need at least a few days notice for the keg. For three or four drinking hours with most guests consuming beer, order a half-keg of beer.

SMOKED SALMON AND BOURSIN IN CUCUMBER CUPS

Approximately 24 appetizers

A tasty and refreshing combination. The salmon is stretched far!

1 large cucumber, peeled and sliced into ½-inch rounds
½ pound herbed Boursin cheese

2 ounces smoked salmon, cut into thin strips about 1¼" x ¼"
fresh parsley or dill

With a spoon or paring knife, cut shallow cup in top of each cucumber round. Wrap cucumbers in paper towels and refrigerate overnight to remove excess moisture. Fill each round with cheese, spreading almost to edge and mounding slightly. Crisscross with 2 strips of salmon and place small sprig of parsley in center. Arrange on platter, cover, and refrigerate until ready to serve.

STUFFED FRENCH BREAD

Approximately 40 thin slices

A hearty and pretty hors d'oeuvre; better if made a day or two in advance.

1 large loaf crusty French
  bread, unsliced
2 8-ounce packages cream
  cheese, softened
¼ cup beer
¼ cup chopped watercress

¼ cup chopped onion
¼ cup chopped radishes
1 tablespoon dry mustard
8 ounces liverwurst, cut
  into small cubes

Preheat oven to 350°.

Cut bread vertically into 3 pieces. Remove ends. Scoop out center to make tubes, leaving about ¼ inch of crusty shell. Crumble the scooped out bread and toast on cookie sheet for 15 minutes. Stir cream cheese until smooth and soft. Stir in beer, watercress, onion, radishes, and mustard. Gently fold in liverwurst cubes and toasted bread. Pack into bread tubes. Wrap in aluminum foil and refrigerate at least 4 hours or overnight. To serve, unwrap and slice as thin as possible.

SWEET BRIE AND CRACKERS

24 servings

A very easy and delicious appetizer. Use a pretty porcelain quiche dish to heat and serve this. Place a basket of crackers next to dish.

1 8-inch round Brie (about
  24 ounces), not fully
  ripened, top rind removed

1 cup chopped pecans
2 cups brown sugar,
  firmly packed

Preheat broiler.

Place Brie in 10-inch quiche dish or pie plate and sprinkle with nuts. Cover top and sides with sugar, patting gently with fingertips. Do not be concerned if sides are not fully covered. Broil on lowest rack until sugar bubbles and melts, about 3 minutes. Serve immediately with crackers.

BOURBON HOT DOGS

30–40 pieces

An easy way to serve good hot dogs.

1 16-ounce package
  frankfurters
½ cup Bourbon whiskey

½ cup brown sugar, firmly
  packed
¼ cup catsup

Slice frankfurters into 4 pieces each. In a small saucepan, combine the Bourbon, catsup, and brown sugar and simmer until sugar is dissolved. Add the meat and pour into a chafing dish and serve.

CHICKEN, SHRIMP, AND ARTICHOKE CASSEROLE

15 servings

This is the answer for a large dinner party. It can be assembled the night before. Double the recipe for twenty-four people.

2 pounds small mushrooms
½ stick butter
5 whole chicken breasts,
  cooked, boned, and cut
  into 1½-2-inch pieces
3 pounds shrimp, boiled
  and peeled, or 3 pounds
  cooked and cleaned
  shrimp
3 14-ounce cans artichoke
  hearts in water, drained
  and quartered

1½ tablespoons Worcestershire
  sauce
¾ cups sherry or dry
  white wine
½ cup freshly grated
  Parmesan cheese

White Sauce:

2/3 cup butter
2/3 cup all-purpose flour
4 cups milk
1 teaspoon salt
⅛ teaspoon nutmeg
¼ teaspoon pepper

Sauté mushrooms in butter. Prepare White Sauce; add Worcestershire and wine. *Preheat oven to 375°.* Place chicken, shrimp, artichokes, and mushrooms in a greased 3-quart (9″ x 13″) casserole. Pour sauce over casserole. Top with cheese. Bake uncovered for 40 minutes, or until bubbly.
White Sauce: Melt butter in a saucepan over low heat. Stir in the flour and use a whisk to blend thoroughly. Add milk and seasonings and cook, stirring constantly, until sauce is thick and smooth.

SLOW COOKER PILAF

12 servings

This is so easy and flavorful. You'll need an electric slow cooker, a great help when entertaining. You may wish to use the slow cooker insert to serve in. You can triple the recipe and put it into two large molds for twenty-four people.

8 ounces mushrooms, sliced
1 onion, chopped
½ stick butter
2 cups long-grain rice

2 cans beef bouillon
1 teaspoon salt
1 cup water
1 teaspoon oregano

Sauté mushrooms and onion in butter in skillet. Add all ingredients to slow cooker and stir. Cook on high for 3 hours. Disconnect the cooker, but do not remove cover. Rice will stay hot and fluffy 2–3 hours.

STRAWBERRY AND BANANA MOLD

8 servings

This is a sweet mold with zip. You can triple the recipe and make two large molds for twenty-four people.

1 16-ounce package frozen strawberries
water
1 6-ounce package cherry gelatin

mashed bananas (2 or 3)
1 20-ounce can crushed pineapple
2 tablespoons lemon juice
1 cup sour cream

Thaw strawberries, reserving juice. To juice, add enough water to make 2 cups. Heat the liquid and in it dissolve the gelatin. Let cool and add all ingredients except sour cream. Pour half the mixture into a ring mold which has been rinsed with cold water and sprayed with vegetable oil. Chill until firm. Spread sour cream on top. Pour remaining gelatin mixture over all and refrigerate.

HERBED MONKEY BREAD

100 miniature rolls

A different and very good way to serve rolls. Easy and better if assembled one day ahead. Guests pull the tiny rolls from the ring. Also delicious as a coffee cake made with one cup of sugar, one tablespoon cinnamon and one-half cup chopped walnuts instead of herbs.

5 7½-ounce tubes
refrigerated buttermilk
biscuits

1½ sticks butter, melted

¼ cup chopped fresh parsley

2 tablespoons chopped fresh chives or scallion tops

1 tablespoon dried dill weed

Cut each biscuit in half vertically. Combine remaining ingredients and blend well. Dip each biscuit into butter mixture, coating thoroughly. Layer biscuits in 12-cup ring mold. Cover and refrigerate overnight. To bake, *preheat oven to 350°*, set mold on foil-lined baking sheet to catch excess butter, and bake for 35–40 minutes. Unmold on serving platter.

CHEESE CAKE SQUARES

Approximately 40 squares

These are heavenly. Best to make the day before and refrigerate. Serve these squares in 2-inch paper cups on a tray. Any leftover squares will freeze well.

1½ sticks unsalted butter

⅔ cup sugar

1 cup chopped walnuts

2 cups all-purpose flour

¾ cup sugar

3 8-ounce packages
cream cheese

3 eggs

6 tablespoons milk

1½ teaspoons vanilla

Preheat oven to 350°.

Cream butter and the ⅔ cup sugar with mixer or in a food processor; add nuts and flour. Mix with hands to crumbly consistency. Spread two thirds of the mixture in a greased 9″ x 13″ baking pan. Press firmly to cover bottom of pan. Bake for 15 minutes. Cream the ¾ cup sugar and cream cheese. Add eggs, milk and vanilla and beat well. Pour over baked base. Sprinkle reserved crumb mixture on top. Return to oven and bake for 30 minutes. Cool and refrigerate. Cut into small squares.

PRALINE STRIPS

Approximately 54 pieces

Easy enough for children to make; they love them. Adults have also been known to find them irresistible!

graham crackers
(about 12)
2 sticks butter or 1
stick each butter
and margarine

1 cup brown sugar,
firmly packed
1 cup chopped walnuts
or pecans

Preheat oven to 350°.

Grease 15" x 10" x ¾" jelly roll pan. Cover the pan with whole graham crackers. Blend butter and sugar in saucepan over moderate heat. Boil for 2 minutes. Sprinkle nuts over graham crackers. Pour the hot syrup over the nuts. Bake for 15 minutes. Cut into strips approximately 1" x 2" with a pizza cutter or knife while slightly warm.

A VALENTINE'S DAY LUNCHEON

30 people

* Do Ahead
** Freeze

* Pink Sangria
* Marinated Salad
** Spinach Lasagne
* Orange, Avocado, and Onion Salad
** Cheese and Bacon French Bread
** Cherry Brandy Chocolate Pie

Everyone will appreciate your special Valentine's Day touches, starting with the Pink Sangria through to the delicious frozen Cherry Brandy Chocolate Pie. You will not have to make too many decisions on what colors to use and what flowers to buy—the special date makes it easy. Red and pink carnations will be beautiful in a few scattered vases in different rooms as well as in your centerpiece.

PINK SANGRIA

Approximately 24 servings

A light and refreshing beverage for a ladies' gathering. This can be made ahead of time and served from a punch bowl in punch cups or from pitchers into wine glasses with a slice of lemon or orange in each glass. Triple the recipe for thirty people.

4 lemons
4 juice oranges
¾ cup water
2½ cups sugar

6 cups cracked ice
4 cups rosé wine, chilled
1 1-quart bottle club soda

Slice lemons and oranges into thin slices. Remove any seeds. Cut orange slices in half. Place fruit on bottom of punch bowl. In a small saucepan, combine water and sugar. Cook over moderate heat until mixture reaches a boil, stirring constantly. Cool. Add rest of ingredients to punch bowl. Stir with a wooden spoon to blend.

MARINATED SALAD

Approximately 200 pieces

Colorful, easy and delicious. Looks fabulous in a three quart glass bowl.

1 bunch broccoli
1 head cauliflower
8 carrots, peeled and julienned
1 cup commercial Italian
   dressing

1 pint box cherry tomatoes
1 6-ounce can pitted ripe
   olives, drained
1 5¾-ounce jar stuffed green
   olives, drained

Clean broccoli and cauliflower and separate into bite-size flowerets. Combine broccoli, cauliflower and carrots and marinate in dressing overnight in refrigerator. To serve, toss with cherry tomatoes and olives.

SPINACH LASAGNE

Everyone loves Spinach Lasagne, a very economical dish for a large group. This recipe fills one 11¾" x 7½" x 1¾" (or flat 2-quart) baking dish. The recipe can be doubled and put into a 15½" x 9" x 2½" lasagne pan. Make this recipe five times for thirty people. Better if made a day or two in advance.

1 medium onion, chopped
½ green pepper, chopped
2 cloves garlic, minced
2 tablespoons oil
1 28-ounce can tomatoes
1 6-ounce can tomato paste
¼ cup minced parsley
½ teaspoon oregano
1 bay leaf
½ 16-ounce box lasagne
   noodles

1 10-ounce package frozen
   chopped spinach, cooked
   and drained
1 pound ricotta cheese
1 egg
¾ cup freshly grated
   Parmesan cheese
1 teaspoon salt
¼ teaspoon pepper
½ pound mozzarella cheese,
   grated

Sauté onions, green peppers, and garlic in oil until golden, stirring often. Stir in tomatoes, tomato paste, parsley, oregano, and bay leaf. Simmer uncovered for 20 minutes. Cook noodles according to package directions and drain. Combine spinach, ricotta, egg, ¼ cup of Parmesan cheese, salt, and pepper. Spoon a third of the tomato sauce in bottom of 2-quart flat baking pan. Layer a third of the lasagne noodles, half of the spinach-ricotta filling, half the mozzarella and ¼ cup of the Parmesan. Repeat layers using half of the remaining sauce and noodles, and all remaining filling. Top with remaining noodles, sauce, Parmesan and mozzarella. Cover tightly and freeze or refrigerate. Bring to room temperature. *Preheat oven to 350°.* Bake, covered, for 45 minutes; uncover and continue baking for 20 minutes. Let stand a few minutes before cutting to serve.

ORANGE, AVOCADO, AND ONION SALAD

6 servings

Very light and refreshing. The sesame seed goes well in this salad.

Dressing:
- ¼ cup sesame seed
- ¼ cup sugar
- ½ teaspoon paprika
- ¼ teaspoon dry mustard
- ½ teaspoon salt
- ½ teaspoon Worcestershire sauce
- 3 tablespoons grated onion
- 6 cups oil
- 3 cups cider vinegar

- ½ head iceberg lettuce, torn into bite-size pieces
- ½ head romaine lettuce, torn into bite-size pieces
- 1 orange, sectioned and cut into bite-size pieces
- ½ avocado, sliced and drenched in lemon juice
- ½ red onion, sliced

Dressing: Toast the sesame seed in a 200° oven, stirring frequently. Combine sugar, paprika, mustard, salt, Worcestershire, and onion in a large bowl. Add the oil and vinegar gradually, stirring constantly with a wire whisk. Transfer to a large jar, add sesame seed and refrigerate.

Toss with salad greens, oranges, avocados, and onions.

CHEESE AND BACON FRENCH BREAD

Approximately 18 pieces

A very hearty and different way to serve bread. Quadruple recipe for thirty (allow at least two slices per guest).

- 1 long thick loaf French or Italian bread
- 1 stick butter, softened
- 1 small onion, grated
- 2 teaspoons mustard
- 1 tablespoon poppy seed
- 1 8-ounce package sliced Swiss cheese
- 2 slices bacon

Slice the bread almost through to the bottom crust at 1″ intervals. Blend butter, onion, mustard, and poppy seed. Spread mixture on both sides of partially sliced bread. Place a slice of Swiss cheese, cut slightly smaller than the bread, between each slice of bread. Lay bacon across top of length of bread. Wrap securely in aluminum foil. Freeze. Bring to room temperature. *Preheat oven to 400°.* Bake 15–20 minutes, open foil, and bake another 5–10 minutes.

CHERRY BRANDY CHOCOLATE PIE

8–10 servings

Serve this delicious dessert right from the freezer. Recipe may be doubled and frozen in a 9" x 13" serving pan. To make serving easier, cut pieces and refreeze before guests arrive.

24 cream-filled chocolate cookies
½ stick butter, melted
1 7-ounce jar marshmallow cream
⅓ cup cherry brandy
2 tablespoons chopped maraschino cherries

2½ cups heavy cream
1 tablespoon maraschino cherry juice
whole maraschino cherries (optional)

Place cookies in a blender or food processor and spin until all are crumbled. Combine with melted butter. Measure and set aside ¼ cup. Press remaining mixture firmly onto bottom and sides of a 9-inch pie pan. Beat marshmallow cream and brandy together until smooth. Fold in chopped cherries. Beat heavy cream to soft peaks and fold into marshmallow mixture along with cherry juice. Turn into crust. Sprinkle reserved crumbs on top and decorate with whole cherries. Cover and freeze. To serve, cut into wedges.

FOURTH OF JULY
COOK-OUT

* Do Ahead
** Freeze

30 people

* Sangria for a Crowd
* Fabulous Spinach Dip with
  Tortilla Chips and Carrots
** Sausage Pizza Rounds
** Shrimp Balls
* Marinated Flank Steak on
  Buttered Rolls
* Zucchini-Carrot Casserole
* Apricot Mold
** Heavenly Brownies

The whole gang is here to celebrate before going on to fireworks. Start your party early enough for your guests to be off to the fireworks by dark. Buy some red, white, and blue balloons to tie to tree branches and porch railings. Let the kids decorate posts and chairs with crepe paper streamers. Tables and benches would be especially good, but any arrangement for outside is fine since guests will be casually dressed. The menu is filled with favorites for children and adults. Fill a tub with ice and soda cans for the kids to help themselves.

SANGRIA FOR A CROWD

6½ quarts or about 50 punch cups

An easy way to make a large batch. You may wish to add a block of ice or a decorated ice ring.

1 gallon dry white jug-wine
1 quart orange juice
1 cup lemon juice
½ cup sugar
½ cup brandy

¼ cup Cointreau
1 quart club soda
3 oranges, sliced
3 lemons, sliced

Mix and chill wine, orange juice, lemon juice, sugar, brandy, and Cointreau. Pour in punch bowl or large crock. Just before serving, add soda, oranges, and lemons.

FABULOUS VEGETABLE DIP WITH TORTILLA CHIPS AND CARROTS

Approximately 1 quart

Everyone asks for this recipe. It can be refrigerated a few days, and should be made at least a day in advance.

1 10-ounce box frozen chopped spinach, defrosted and squeezed dry
1 8-ounce can water chestnuts, chopped

1 1⅝-ounce package dried vegetable soup mix
2 cups sour cream
2 cups mayonnaise

Combine all ingredients. Refrigerate. Serve with tortilla chips and carrot sticks.

SAUSAGE PIZZA ROUNDS

Approximately 36 canapés

Always a hit. Keep them on hand—just take them out of the freezer and pop them under the broiler.

½ pound bulk sausage
½ pound ground beef
½ pound Cheddar cheese,
  grated
½ teaspoon basil

½ teaspoon oregano
⅛ teaspoon garlic powder
1 tablespoon parsley flakes
1 loaf small party rye bread

Brown sausage and hamburger lightly in skillet. Drain. Add cheese and spices. Stir until melted and blended. Spread on rye bread slices. Freeze on a cookie sheet, place in plastic bags, and store in freezer. To serve, thaw, then broil about 5 minutes, or until bubbly.

SHRIMP BALLS

30 shrimp balls

Very good and just have to be reheated at the last minute.

1 pound shrimp
  water chestnuts, minced
  (8–10)
1 egg

1 teaspoon salt
½ teaspoon sugar
1 teaspoon cornstarch
  oil for deep frying

Shell, devein, and mince the shrimp. Combine shrimp, water chestnuts, egg, salt, sugar, and cornstarch. Drop by heaping teaspoonfuls into hot (375°) oil. When balls turn pink, remove with slotted spoon. Drain on paper towels. Serve immediately. May be made in advance, frozen, and reheated in oven.

MARINATED FLANK STEAK ON BUTTERED ROLLS

6–8 servings

Easy and delicious. Buy really nice rolls which you split and butter. I get snow-flake soft rolls at the bakery. For thirty people, buy about forty-five rolls. You will use six to eight rolls with each steak. Buy six steaks for a group of thirty. Make marinade recipe three times. Marinate steaks in a heavy duty plastic bag.

1½ cups soy sauce
2 tablespoons brown sugar
½ teaspoon ground ginger

½ teaspoon dry mustard
1 2-pound flank steak

Combine first 4 ingredients and pour over flank steak. Marinate about 4 hours. Have meat at room temperature before cooking. Broil approximately 4 minutes on each side. Let stand 15 minutes, then slice diagonally into thin slices. Marinade can be stored in refrigerator for use in the near future.

ZUCCHINI-CARROT CASSEROLE

8 servings

A real favorite. Goes well with any meat, poultry, or fish. Double the recipe twice, using larger casseroles, for thirty people.

2 pounds zucchini, sliced
  into ¾-inch rounds
¼ cup chopped onion
1 cup sour cream
1 can cream of chicken soup,
  undiluted

1 cup shredded carrots
1 8-ounce package seasoned
  bread stuffing
1 stick butter, melted

Cook zucchini and onion in boiling salted water for 5 minutes. Drain. In a bowl, combine sour cream and soup; stir in shredded carrots. Fold in zucchini. Mix stuffing with melted butter. Place half the stuffing in bottom of 11¾″ x 7½″ x 1¾″ baking dish or 2-quart casserole. Cover with zucchini. Top with remaining stuffing. Cover and refrigerate. Bring to room temperature. *Preheat oven to 350°.* Bake for 25–30 minutes.

APRICOT MOLD

10 servings

This looks so pretty and it has such a delicate taste that it is an attractive addition to any table. Make three for thirty people.

1 29-ounce can apricots
1 6-ounce package apricot
  gelatin

1 pint vanilla ice cream,
  softened
1 cup sour cream
  mandarin oranges
  lettuce

Drain the apricots, reserving juice. Discard pits and puree apricots. To juice, add enough water to make 2 cups. Bring to a boil and in it, dissolve gelatin. Cool in refrigerator until syrupy. Add softened ice cream, sour cream, and apricot puree. Pour into an 8-cup mold which has been rinsed with cold water and sprayed with vegetable oil. Refrigerate. To serve, unmold on a platter and garnish with mandarin oranges and lettuce.

HEAVENLY BROWNIES

Approximately 50 brownies

Friends have begged for this recipe. Here it is. Rich and wonderful. For a thicker brownie, use a 13" x 9" baking dish.

4 eggs, beaten
2 cups sugar
1½ cups all-purpose flour
1 teaspoon vanilla
2 sticks butter or 1 stick
  each butter and margarine
⅓ cup unsweetened cocoa
1½ cups chopped pecans or
  walnuts
1 10½-ounce package

miniature marshmallows
(you will not need the
entire bag)
Frosting:
2 teaspoons instant coffee
  powder
⅓ cup milk
1 stick butter, melted
3 tablespoons unsweetened
  cocoa
1 1-pound box powdered sugar

Preheat oven to 350°.

Combine eggs, sugar, flour, and vanilla. Melt butter and add the cocoa. Add to egg mixture and beat well. Bake in greased 10½" x 15" pan for 20–25 minutes, or until toothpick comes out clean. As soon as cake is taken from oven, cover with marshmallows. Return pan to oven until marshmallows are slightly puffed or melted, 6–8 minutes. Sprinkle nuts on top of marshmallow. Pour frosting over nuts.

Frosting: Dissolve coffee powder in milk. Add to butter and cocoa. Beat in sugar until fairly smooth.

NEW YEAR'S EVE COCKTAIL PARTY

■□■□■■□■□■■□■□■□■□■□■□■□■□■□■□■□■□■■□■

35 people

COLD:
* * Champagne Punch
* * Pineapple Shrimp Appetizers with Dip
* * Caviar Ring

HOT:
* ** Chicken Nuggets with Dip
* ** Spinach Cheese Squares
* ** Tiropetes (Cheese-Filled Phyllo Dough Triangles)

This evening deserves the very best. The group is starting the gala night at your place and you want them to enjoy Champagne Punch with this really elegant holiday food. Polish your best silver and hang some paper streamers from helium balloons on your ceiling. The mood is set for a marvelous evening.

CHAMPAGNE PUNCH

For special occasions. Pour into champagne or wine glasses over a thin orange slice.

1 lemon, sliced thin
1 orange, sliced thin
1 quart fresh strawberries
4 jiggers brandy
4 jiggers apricot liqueur

4 fifth-bottles champagne
1 1-quart bottle club soda
2 oranges, sliced thin and
halved

Pour all ingredients except halved orange slices over a block of ice or decorated ice ring in a punch bowl. Stir and ladle into glasses.

PINEAPPLE SHRIMP APPETIZERS WITH DIP

Approximately 70 appetizers

This is an attractive and absolutely delicious treat. The shrimp goes further because of the fresh pineapple bits. I always buy Hawaiian pineapples—they are sweeter and juicier. They cost more but they're worth every penny. Get the shrimp that, when cleaned and cooked, come to about 25–30 per pound. Plan on about 2½ per person. You don't want your guests to make a meal of them since they are so expensive, so don't put this out at the beginning of your party—wait awhile.

1 large pineapple
2½ pounds cleaned and
cooked shrimp
frilled colored toothpicks
1 bunch leaf lettuce

Dip:

2 cups mayonnaise
1 cup seafood cocktail
sauce
2 tablespoons lemon juice
1 tablespoon horseradish
or to taste

Halve the pineapple, leaving the leaves attached to one half. Scoop fruit out carefully with a grapefruit knife. Cut fruit into small cubes. Pare other half and cut fruit into cubes. (Discard the hard inside core.) Put cubes in a bowl and cover tightly. Drain the pineapple shell and refrigerate in a plastic bag. Mix all the dip ingredients and refrigerate. This may be done a day ahead. When ready to assemble, spear a piece of pineapple and a shrimp on each toothpick. Place the pineapple half on a bed of lettuce leaves surrounded by the shrimp on toothpicks. Fill pineapple with dip, cover with plastic wrap, and refrigerate until ready to serve.

CAVIAR RING

This is a very festive mold that can be made a few days ahead. It looks lovely with the center filled with black olives. Stoned wheat crackers or toasted extra-thin white bread cut into thin points are both good accompaniments. Double all ingredients except olives to serve thirty-five people with this menu.

6 hard-cooked eggs
1 8-ounce package cream cheese, at room temperature
3-4 scallions, sliced, including 1 inch of green tops

salt to taste
1 2-ounce jar salmon caviar
1 6-ounce can black pitted olives, drained
parsley

Thoroughly blend eggs, cream cheese, scallions, and salt in a food processor. Pour into a 6-cup (or smaller) ring mold which has been rinsed with cold water and sprayed with vegetable oil. Refrigerate. Unmold onto a serving platter. With a spoon or spatula, slightly flatten top of ring. Spoon caviar on top all around. Some will slide down. Fill cavity with black olives. Arrange some parsley around mold.

CHICKEN NUGGETS WITH DIP

Approximately 120 nuggets

This is exceptional. Make a lot, because these delightful morsels will be gobbled right up. If you're pressed for time, Chicken Nuggets may be reheated when partially defrosted. Plan on at least three per person.

2 cups Bisquick
2 eggs
1 cup milk
1 tablespoon garlic salt
   pepper
   oil for deep frying
4 large whole chicken
   breasts, skinned, boned,

and cut into bite-size
pieces, approximately 1"
square

Dip:
4 tablespoons very hot
   Dijon-style mustard
1½ cups orange marmalade

Combine Bisquick, egg, milk, garlic salt, and pepper and blend well. Heat oil to 365° in a deep fryer or electric fry pan. Dip chicken pieces into batter and fry until golden brown. Remove with a slotted spoon to a pan lined with newspaper and then paper towels. When cool, remove to a container for freezing. Defrost on cookie sheet in single layer. To reheat, *preheat oven to 350°*. Bake for 8 minutes, or until heated through.

Dip: Combine mustard and marmalade and heat slightly. Serve Chicken Nuggets with Dip and toothpicks.

SPINACH CHEESE SQUARES

40–50 squares

This is a winner every time. The squares are like crustless quiches and they are easy to prepare. Try making them on a disposable cookie sheet, 15" x 10" x ¾", and freezing without removing them from the pan. Just use a dull knife when cutting into pieces so you do not puncture the pan.

4 tablespoons butter
3 eggs
1 cup all-purpose flour
1 cup milk
1 teaspoon salt
1 teaspoon baking powder

1 pound Monterey Jack
   cheese, grated
4 cups chopped fresh spinach,
   or 2 10-ounce packages
   frozen chopped spinach,
   thawed and well drained

Preheat oven to 350°.

In a 9" x 13" x 2" baking dish, melt butter in oven. In a large mixing bowl, beat eggs; add flour, milk, salt, and baking powder. Mix well. Stir in cheese and spinach. Spread in pan and bake for 35 minutes. Cool 30–40 minutes, then cut into squares. Refrigerate or freeze. To serve, bring to room temperature, *preheat oven to 350°*, and reheat the squares for about 10 minutes.

TIROPETES (CHEESE-FILLED PHYLLO DOUGH TRIANGLES)

Approximately 80 pieces

These flaky little triangles taste fantastic. They can be made weeks in advance and frozen. Baking time is only one minute longer if they are placed in the oven right from the freezer. Best to refrigerate filling a few hours or overnight before making the triangles.

2 **tablespoons butter**	1 **pound feta cheese,**
2 **tablespoons all-purpose**	**crumbled**
flour	1 **1-pound box phyllo dough**
2 **cups milk**	**(See p. 7)**
4 **eggs, slightly beaten**	1 **pound butter, melted**

In a saucepan, melt the 2 tablespoons of butter and add the flour to form a paste. Add milk and stir until smooth. Add eggs and feta cheese, stirring and cooking until thick (about 5 minutes). Cool and refrigerate.

Take phyllo dough out of refrigerator about 2 hours before you start making triangles. Open a package of dough and cut ½ inch off end of plastic sleeve. Carefully slide out a few inches of the dough from the sleeve and, with a sharp knife, cut through entire pastry roll about 1½ inches from end. Replace bulk of dough in sleeve and close end securely with a twist so dough will not dry out. Unfold cut dough and put next to your working area. Take 2 strips and brush each with melted butter, stacking one on top of the other. Take ½ teaspoon of the cheese mixture and place at bottom end of strip. Fold into triangles (as if folding a flag).

Hint: When starting to fold triangle, enclose cheese mixture entirely with dough so that the filling will not come out when baking. Repeat with the rest of the strips, brushing tops with butter. Freeze, using wax paper to divide layers. When thoroughly frozen, remove to plastic bags and store in freezer. *Preheat oven to 350°*. Bake for 20 minutes, or until puffy and lightly browned. Wait 5 minutes before serving, since filling will be extremely hot.

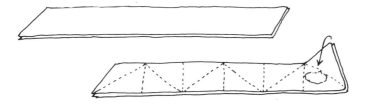

CHRISTMAS EVE BUFFET DINNER

50 people

* Do Ahead
** Freeze

* **Hot Wine Cheer**
* **Easy Shrimp and Cheese Fondue**
** **Sauerkraut Balls**
** **Chicken Divan**
   or
** **Chicken Tetrazzini**
* **Shredded Carrot Casserole**
* **Tossed Salad with Tomatoes**
* **Buttered Rolls**
* **Phyllo Nut Rolls**

The feeling that comes over a house on Christmas Eve with the house decorated, presents wrapped, and lights on the tree is a very special and peaceful one. The Hot Wine Cheer fills your home with spicy fragrance perfect for this occasion. Buy a bright red tablecloth if you do not already own one. You will find many uses for it and you will love having it when Christmas rolls around each year. If you have a piano, make sure someone can play carols. Ask musician friends to bring their instruments and hand around some Christmas song sheets so everyone can sing.

HOT WINE CHEER

10 cups

Especially nice around the holidays in cold weather. Triple the recipe for fifty people.

½ cup sugar
1 cup water
10 cloves
3 cinnamon sticks
¼ teaspoon allspice

1 orange, sliced
1 lemon, sliced
1 46-ounce can pineapple juice
1 fifth Burgundy

Combine all ingredients except Burgundy in a pot on the stove. Cover and heat slowly for at least 1 hour. Fifteen minutes before serving, add Burgundy and turn off heat. Let sit until ready to serve so punch cups will not break.

EASY CHEESE AND SHRIMP FONDUE

12 servings

Easy, and everyone loves it. This can be prepared ahead and reheated just before serving. The bread may also be cut into chunks and frozen or refrigerated in bags until needed. Triple recipe for fifty people.

1 10¾-ounce can of cream of shrimp soup
½ pound Swiss cheese, grated

2 tablespoons white wine
French bread

Combine all ingredients except bread in a double boiler and heat until cheese melts. Serve in a chafing dish or fondue pot along with hunks of French bread for dunking.

SAUERKRAUT BALLS

Approximately 60 balls

A very good appetizer that can be frozen after cooking. Just reheat to serve. Double the recipe for fifty people.

¾ cup chopped onion
2¼ pounds crumbled sausage meat
1 pound sauerkraut, drained and chopped
5 tablespoons fresh bread crumbs
1 8-ounce package cream cheese, at room temperature

5 tablespoons chopped parsley
3 teaspoons mustard
¼ teaspoon garlic salt freshly ground pepper
1 cup all-purpose flour
2 eggs, well beaten
¼ cup milk
1½ cups fine dry bread crumbs oil for deep frying

Sauté onion and sausage in a skillet until sausage is brown. Drain. Add sauerkraut and fresh bread crumbs. Combine cream cheese, parsley, mustard, garlic salt, and pepper. Stir into sauerkraut mixture. Chill. Shape into 1-inch balls and coat with flour. Combine eggs and milk. Dip balls into egg-milk mixture and roll in bread crumbs. Deep fry in very hot oil until brown. To serve, *preheat oven to 375°*. Bake for 15 minutes.

CHICKEN DIVAN

10 servings

This is a wonderful dish for almost any occasion. It is an easy-to-make casserole but a very elegant one. It's hearty, yet delicate. Make four or five casseroles for fifty people, depending on how many other dishes you will be serving with it. Can be frozen or made two days in advance and refrigerated.

3 packages frozen broccoli spears or cut broccoli, cooked and drained

5 large whole chicken breasts, cooked, boned, and cut into 2-inch chunks

2 cans cream of chicken soup, undiluted

1 cup mayonnaise

1½ tablespoons lemon juice

1½ teaspoons curry powder

6 ounces sharp Cheddar cheese, grated

4 slices firm textured white bread, crusts removed melted butter

Preheat oven to 350°.

In a buttered 13″ x 9″ baking dish, layer broccoli, then chicken pieces. Combine soup, mayonnaise, lemon juice, and curry powder and pour over chicken. Spread cheese evenly over soup mixture. Cut bread into 1-inch squares, dip into melted butter and arrange on top. Bake for 25–30 minutes. The casserole may be frozen, brought to room temperature, and then baked.

CHICKEN TETRAZZINI

12 servings

Everyone loves this very delicate chicken dish. Make it a few days ahead. Cook and cut the chicken one day and finish preparing the dish the following day. If you are going to make four casseroles for this menu, it won't seem like such a large task this way.

2 3-pound broiler-fryer
  chickens
1 onion
  celery tops
  salt and pepper
1 16-ounce package spaghetti
1 stick butter
1 bunch scallions, chopped,
  including 1 inch of green
  tops

8 ounces mushrooms, sliced
1 tablespoon lemon juice
½ cup all-purpose flour
2 teaspoons salt
½ teaspoon nutmeg
½ cup sherry or dry white
  wine
1 cup half-and-half
4 ounces freshly grated
  Parmesan cheese

Place chickens in hot water with onion, celery tops, salt, and pepper and simmer for 45 minutes. Cool in stock. Remove skin and cut chicken meat into thin 2″ long strips. Reserve 3½ cups of the broth.

Break spaghetti in half and cook according to directions on package. Rinse thoroughly with cold water and drain.

Grease a 13″ x 9″ baking dish.

In a medium-sized saucepan, melt 2 tablespoons butter. Add scallions, mushrooms, and lemon juice and sauté 7 minutes. With slotted spoon, place mixture in a bowl. In same pan, melt remaining butter. Add flour, salt, and nutmeg, stirring until smooth. Raise heat and gradually stir in sherry and reserved chicken broth, stirring constantly, until it reaches a boil. Turn off heat and add half-and-half. In a large container, mix the sauce with cooked spaghetti, mushroom mixture, and chicken. Mix well with hands or large spoon. Put in greased baking dish. Sprinkle top with cheese, cover tightly, and freeze.

Bring to room temperature. *Preheat oven to 350°.* Bake uncovered for 25–30 minutes, or until bubbly.

SHREDDED CARROT CASSEROLE

6 servings

Very easy, and it complements a variety of main dishes.

3 tablespoons butter
¼ cup chopped onion
6 carrots, peeled and
   shredded

¾ teaspoon salt
1 teaspoon sugar
½ cup water or chicken
   stock

Preheat oven to 350°.

Melt butter in a heat-proof casserole and sauté onion for 3 minutes. Add carrots and stir to coat. Sprinkle with salt and sugar. Pour water or stock over carrots. Cover. Bake for 35 minutes.

PHYLLO NUT ROLLS

Approximately 45 nut rolls

These buttery little pastries taste like baklava but they are less rich and can be eaten as a finger food. Can be made a day or two ahead. Delicious. A little time consuming to make, but rather easy! Plan to make this recipe twice for fifty people.

Nut Rolls:

1½ cups ground walnuts
   or almonds
3 tablespoons sugar
2 teaspoons cinnamon
1 teaspoon powdered cloves
1 1-pound box phyllo dough
   (See p. 7)
1 pound butter, melted

Syrup:

1 cup water
1 cup sugar
¼ cup honey
½ teaspoon lemon juice
   few pieces of lemon or
   orange rind
1 small cinnamon stick

Nut Rolls: Combine nuts, sugar, and spices in a bowl. Cut end of plastic sleeve. Slide out just enough dough to slice off one third of the roll. Slide unused dough back into sleeve and twist plastic end to prevent air from drying it out. Next to a cutting board or work area, unroll the one-third section. Place one strip on the cutting board and brush generously with butter. Layer with another strip and brush with butter. Place 1 teaspoon of filling at bottom of narrow end of strip. Turn in sides and roll over to form a roll approximately 2 inches long. Repeat with the rest of the dough. Put in a jelly roll pan, seam side down, so they do not touch. Brush tops with butter. *Preheat oven to 325°.* Bake for 20–25 minutes, or until golden brown. Remove from oven and pour syrup evenly over rolls. Cover pan lightly with aluminum foil until syrup is absorbed (overnight).

Syrup: Combine all ingredients, bring to a boil, and cook for 10 minutes.

MEMORIAL DAY COCKTAIL PARTY AND A CASSEROLE FOR HANGERS-ON

■ ■

75 people

* Do Ahead
* * Freeze

	* Piña Coladas
COLD:	* Chicken Bites
	* Ham Roll-ups
	* Egg Salad Pinwheel Sandwiches
HOT:	* * Cheese Delights
	* Artichoke Quiche
	* * Mushroom Turnovers
LATER	* * Hot Chicken Salad Casserole
	* * Rolls
	* Tossed Salad
	Coffee

The first long weekend of the season is coming up and you're in the mood for a big party to herald the long relaxing summer days ahead. You are inviting seventy-five people for cocktails, and you expect that some will stay beyond the cocktail hour. If the weather is warm, plan to move some or all of your party outside. Memorial Day is a patriotic holiday, so fly your flag from a flagpole or drape it at the windows. Try Piña Coladas for an exotic salute to summer.

PIÑA COLADAS

4 servings

A very popular tropical drink. Have a blender ready. Instead of pineapple strips, you may wish to substitute 4 pineapple chunks per serving.

6 ounces (¾ cup) light rum
½ cup coconut cream or
  Piña Colada mix

2 cups pineapple juice
  crushed ice
  pineapple sticks

Place first three ingredients in blender. Add crushed ice until three quarters full. Blend until frothy. Garnish with stick of fresh pineapple.

CHICKEN BITES

Approximately 30 pieces

The chicken is coated with an unusual and spicy sauce. Pile it in the center of a platter and surround with lettuce leaves. Dot with parsley and capers and serve with toothpicks. Double or triple the recipe for this menu.

1 large whole chicken
  breast, skinned and boned
½ cup sour cream
¼ cup mayonnaise
2 teaspoons chili sauce
1 tablespoon horseradish
1½ teaspoons Worcestershire
  sauce

1 tablespoon lemon juice
⅛ teaspoon Tabasco
½ teaspoon curry powder
1 tablespoon chutney,
  minced fine
2 tablespoons capers
1 tablespoon chopped
  parsley

Preheat oven to 400°.

Cut chicken breasts into bite-size pieces and place in buttered jelly roll pan. Cover with a sheet of wax paper and bake in oven for 8 minutes. They are done when they spring back when pressed with a finger. Combine remaining ingredients, mix well, and add chicken. Refrigerate several hours or overnight.

HAM ROLL-UPS

Approximately 28 pieces

These look very pretty arranged alternately with other hors d'oeuvres. They can be made a few days in advance and kept in a tightly covered container in the refrigerator.

2 8-ounce packages cream
  cheese
1 tablespoon horseradish

1 1-pound package thinly
  sliced ham
  minced parsley

Combine cream cheese and horseradish—make it pretty hot. Spread mixture on each piece of ham. Roll lengthwise and cut into four pieces. Dip each end into minced parsley.

EGG SALAD PINWHEEL SANDWICHES

Approximately 70 sandwiches

These look so professional and they taste great. You will probably have to order the 15-inch pullman loaf the day before from your bakery. The bread must be very fresh.

1 long (about 15″) loaf
  unsliced white bread
8 hard-cooked eggs, riced
¼ cup mayonnaise, or to taste
  salt and pepper to taste

butter or margarine,
softened
sweet large gherkin pickles,
cut in half

Slice the bread horizontally into 7 workable slices. Combine eggs, mayonnaise, salt, and pepper and refrigerate until ready to assemble. You might want to use your rolling pin lightly on the pieces of bread. The softer and more pliable the bread, the less you'll need a rolling pin. Lay the slices side by side (two or three at a time) and cut each slice in half crosswise. Spread butter at the top of each piece (so it will stay closed when rolled). Spread the rest of each slice with egg mixture. Place a pickle across the bottom of each piece of bread parallel with the bottom. Starting with the pickle end, roll each piece and wrap a piece of wax paper around like a party snapper—make sure the twists at the ends are tight. Wrap loosely in a wet paper towel, place in a plastic bag, and refrigerate overnight or at least a few hours. Slice each roll into approximately 5 slices.

CHEESE DELIGHTS

These are wonderful and very substantial party fare. Keep the recipe in mind when last-minute company comes, too. They may be frozen, then thawed and broiled.

6 plain or onion English muffins
butter
4 ounces sharp Cheddar cheese, grated

4 ounces mozzarella cheese, grated
¾ cup mayonnaise
1 cup pitted ripe olives, chopped fine

Cut the muffins in half and butter lightly. Make a paste of the cheeses, mayonnaise, and olives. Spread on muffin halves and cut into quarters. Preheat broiler. Broil until bubbly and light golden brown.

ARTICHOKE QUICHE

40 serving squares

A very tasty crustless quiche. Double (or triple) the recipe for seventy-five people.

2 6-ounce jars marinated artichoke hearts
6 scallions, chopped, or 1 small onion, chopped fine
1 clove garlic, chopped
4 eggs
¼ cup fine dry bread crumbs

½ pound Cheddar cheese, grated
2 tablespoons chopped parsley
¼ teaspoon oregano
⅛ teaspoon Tabasco
¼ teaspoon salt

Preheat oven to 325°.

Drain artichokes, saving marinade from 1 jar. In reserved marinade, sauté scallions and garlic. Cut artichokes into small pieces. Beat eggs, add artichokes, scallions, garlic, and all remaining ingredients. Turn into a greased 7″ x 11″ baking pan. Bake for 30 minutes. Let cool a little before cutting into serving pieces.

MUSHROOM TURNOVERS

These tender, savory little pastries are always a hit. Double recipe for seventy-five people.

Pastry:
- 3 3-ounce packages cream cheese, at room temperature
- ½ cup butter, softened
- 1½ cups all-purpose flour
- ½ teaspoon salt

Filling:
- 3 tablespoons butter
- 1 large onion, chopped fine
- 8 ounces mushrooms, chopped
- ¼ teaspoon thyme
- ½ teaspoon salt
- ½ teaspoon pepper
- 2 tablespoons all-purpose flour
- ¼ cup sour cream
- 1 egg
- 1 teaspoon milk

Pastry: Blend cream cheese and butter thoroughly. Add flour and salt and work until smooth. Chill well for at least 30 minutes. Roll dough out to ⅛-inch thickness on lightly floured surface and cut into rounds with a 3-inch biscuit cutter.

In a skillet, heat butter, add onion, and brown. Add mushrooms and cook, stirring often, about 3 minutes. Add seasonings and sprinkle with flour. Stir in sour cream and cook gently until thickened. *Preheat oven to 450°.* Place 1 teaspoon filling on each round and fold dough over. Press edges together with a fork. Pinch top crust. Place on greased cookie sheet. Brush tops with 1 egg, lightly beaten, mixed with 1 teaspoon milk. Bake 10–15 minutes, or until lightly browned. Turnovers may be frozen, then thawed before baking.

HOT CHICKEN SALAD CASSEROLE

10 servings

This is a wonderful casserole. It is filling, different, and a blessing for a hostess when guests stay on—and on. It will not be necessary to make enough Hot Chicken Salad Casserole for all your cocktail party guests. Chances are only about a quarter of them will linger if they have been invited just for cocktails. The recipe can be doubled. If you plan to freeze, omit the eggs.

1 cup rice
4 cups chopped cooked
  chicken
1 can cream of chicken soup,
  undiluted
1 small onion, chopped
½ teaspoon salt
2 teaspoons lemon juice

¾ cup chopped celery
1 can water chestnuts,
  chopped
½ cup mayonnaise
2 hard-cooked eggs, chopped
8 ounces Cheddar cheese,
  grated

Cook rice according to package directions, then rinse with cold water. Combine all ingredients except cheese and mix well. Spoon into a greased oven-proof casserole. Top with grated cheese, and refrigerate. *Preheat oven to 350°.* Bake for 35 minutes.

NEW YEAR'S DAY OPEN HOUSE

100 people

* Do Ahead
** Freeze

COLD:
* Holiday Punch
* Marinated Broccoli and Dip
* Stuffed Mushrooms

HOT:
** Pizza Appetizers
** Cheese Puffs
** Shrimp Toast
** Zucchini Savories

BUFFET TABLE:
* Baked Ham
* A Variety of Mustards
** Miniature Buttermilk Biscuits
* Cheese Boat
* Hot Beef Spread in Chafing Dish
** Roasted Pecans

Your guests will know they are at a special party the minute they enter your home. The intriguing aroma from your Holiday Punch will set the tone for a cheery New Year's open house. The punch should be easily accessible to arriving guests. Have your children or hired teenagers pass trays of beautifully arranged food. Your self-service punch bowl eliminates the need for one bartender. If you decide to have an open bar, too, set it up in another area. It would be best to have a bartender for such a large crowd, though guests can help themselves if there is someone appointed to keep the bar well stocked and tidy.

HOLIDAY PUNCH

40–50 servings

Party-goers love this. The spicy Christmas-time odor is fabulous and the punch is guaranteed to make conversation sparkle! Serve hot in a large crock or silver punch bowl. A glass punch bowl might break. Make the punch three or four times for a hundred people, as your guests will probably be arriving at different times for an open house party.

3 pieces fresh gingerroot
2 sticks cinnamon
8 whole cloves
4 cardamom seeds
6 lemons

6 juice oranges
1 gallon apple cider
1 quart pineapple juice
½ teaspoon salt
rum

Tie spices in a bag of fine cheesecloth. Peel and cut the lemons and oranges into thin slices and add to the combined cider and pineapple juice. To this mixture add the spice bag and bring to a very low simmering boil. Stir as it simmers for 15 minutes. Add the salt, stirring vigorously. Prior to serving, add as much rum as desired.

MARINATED BROCCOLI AND DIP

10 servings

Listen for raves about this combination of color, texture, and flavor. Do not use wine vinegar. It will dim the bright green of the broccoli. For this menu, prepare six or seven bunches of broccoli and triple the marinade and the dip.

1 large bunch fresh broccoli

Marinade:
¼ cup cider or white vinegar
¾ cup salad oil
2 cloves garlic, split
1½ teaspoons sugar
2 teaspoons fresh dill

Dip:
1 cup mayonnaise
1½ tablespoons curry powder
1 tablespoon catsup
¼ teaspoon Worcestershire sauce

Cut broccoli into flowerets with 1½-inch stems. Split the large pieces to make them bite size. Combine ingredients for marinade in a jar and shake well. Put cut broccoli in a medium-size plastic bag and pour over marinade. Seal bag and refrigerate up to a day before serving. Mix ingredients for dip and refrigerate. Drain broccoli and serve with dip.

STUFFED MUSHROOMS

50 appetizers

This a tangy, flavorful combination.

50 small- to medium-size mushrooms
1 cup blue cheese
1 cup Camembert cheese
1 cup ground walnuts
2 teaspoons Worcestershire sauce
1½ teaspoons curry powder

Clean the mushrooms. Remove stems. Cream the cheeses together. Blend in the nuts, Worcestershire, and curry. Fill the caps with mixture. Chill and serve cold.

PIZZA APPETIZERS

Approximately 48 appetizers

A good recipe for a large party. These little pizzas may be baked when partially defrosted.

1 pound bulk pork sausage
2 tablespoons butter
1 cup chopped onions
1½ cups shredded Cheddar cheese
½ cup grated Parmesan cheese
1½ teaspoons oregano
1 teaspoon garlic salt
1 6-ounce can tomato paste
1 8-ounce can tomato sauce
2 8-ounce tubes butterflake dinner rolls
shredded mozzarella cheese

Crumble and sauté sausage in butter until partially cooked. Add onions and cook until onions are soft and sausage is done. Drain off excess fat. Add Cheddar, Parmesan, oregano, garlic salt, tomato paste, and tomato sauce. Simmer 20 minutes and cool. Remove dough from tubes and separate the 12 sections into 3 or 4 layers each. Place on cookie sheets. Put 1 teaspoon pizza mix on each layer. Freeze on cookie sheets. When frozen, carefully remove and store in plastic containers in the freezer. To serve, *preheat oven to 400°*. Top pizzas liberally with mozzarella. Bake on cookie sheet for 10 minutes.

CHEESE PUFFS

48 appetizers

A good recipe for a large crowd. Or make a batch and pop them from the freezer at the last minute for unexpected guests or as a treat for your family. Double or triple this recipe for a hundred people. Cheese Puffs may be baked when partially defrosted.

1 1-pound loaf firm white bread, unsliced
1 stick butter
¼ cup diced mozzarella cheese
¼ cup grated sharp Cheddar cheese
¼ cup grated Swiss cheese
1 3-ounce package cream cheese
½ teaspoon dry mustard
⅛ teaspoon cayenne pepper
  salt to taste
2 egg whites

Trim crusts from top, bottom, and sides of the loaf. Cut the bread into 1-inch cubes and set aside. In a saucepan, combine butter and all the cheeses and stir over moderate heat until thoroughly blended. Add mustard, cayenne, and salt. Beat the egg whites until stiff and fold them into the cheese mixture. Using a two-tined fork, spear the bread cubes one at a time and dip them into the mixture until well coated. Arrange the cubes on a baking sheet and immediately freeze until firm. Remove the cubes from baking sheet and store in plastic bags in freezer. To serve, *preheat oven to 400°*. Place cubes on cookie sheet and bake for 10 minutes, or until lightly browned.

SHRIMP TOAST

You'll find that a pound of shrimp goes a long way with these crunchy little morsels. They are a real favorite. Double (at least) for a hundred people.

5 ounces water chestnuts, drained	2 teaspoons salt
1 pound raw, cleaned, shelled shrimp	1 teaspoon sugar
	1 egg, beaten
¼ cup chopped scallion tops	15 slices very thin white bread
1 teaspoon minced gingerroot	fine, dry bread crumbs
	oil

In a blender or food processor, puree water chestnuts, shrimp, scallions, and ginger. Mix in salt, sugar, and egg. Remove crusts from bread and spread paste on one side of each slice. Sprinkle with crumbs. Cut each slice into 4 triangles. In an electric fry pan, heat 1 inch of oil to 375° and fry each triangle, shrimp side down, then turn and brown other side, frying about 2 minutes on each side. Remove with a slotted spoon and drain on paper towels. Store in freezer. To serve, thaw the toast. *Preheat oven to 400°.* Place toasts upside down on a rack and heat for 5 minutes.

ZUCCHINI SAVORIES

You will like this for a good-size group. The flavor is great. Make the recipe twice for a hundred people.

3 cups grated zucchini (3 or 4)	½ teaspoon salt
1 cup Bisquick	½ teaspoon seasoned salt
½ cup chopped onion	½ teaspoon oregano
½ cup grated Parmesan cheese	dash pepper
	1 clove garlic, chopped
2 tablespoons chopped parsley	½ cup vegetable oil
	4 eggs

Preheat oven to 350°.

Mix all ingredients thoroughly and place in a buttered 13″ x 9″ pan. Bake 25 minutes. Cut into bite-size pieces. Serve warm. If frozen, thaw and reheat at 350° for 5–10 minutes.

BAKED HAM

A large baked ham, its surface divided into diamond shapes centered with whole cloves, is an impressive focal point for any table. It will feed a large crowd and cost very little of your time in preparation. Just allow the ham enough time for sitting, baking, and more sitting. With all the other food on this menu, one large ham is enough. The frequent basting gives a very tempting flavor.

1 precooked boned ham (18–20 pounds)
whole cloves
1½ cups brown sugar, firmly packed

2 cups pineapple juice
2 cups fresh or canned diced pineapple
2 tablespoons mustard
beer

Leave ham at room temperature for 6–7 hours. *Preheat oven to 350°.* Slash the skin diagonally to create a diamond pattern. Place a clove in the center of each diamond. Puree in blender the sugar, pineapple juice, diced pineapple, and mustard. Place ham on a rack in roasting pan. Pour pineapple mixture over ham. Bake for 1 hour. Reduce heat to 300° and bake another 2 hours. As juice in pan boils down, add beer. Baste ham every 15 minutes, adding beer as needed. Remove the rack for the last 30 minutes of cooking and place ham directly in the sauce on the bottom of the roasting pan. Cover with pan drippings before serving. This can sit for hours. Surround the platter with small dishes of different kinds of mustard.

MINIATURE BUTTERMILK BISCUITS

Pile a basket high with split and buttered biscuits and place it next to the ham. Figure on one and a half or two biscuits per person. If you want smaller biscuits, use a smaller cutter. They can be split, buttered, wrapped, and frozen.

2 cups all-purpose flour	1 teaspoon salt
2 teaspoons baking powder	½ stick butter
¼ teaspoon baking soda	¾ cup buttermilk

Preheat oven to 450°.

In a large bowl, with fork, mix flour, baking powder, baking soda, and salt. With pastry blender or 2 knives used scissor-fashion, cut in butter until mixture resembles coarse crumbs; add buttermilk. With fork, quickly mix just until mixture forms soft dough that leaves sides of bowl.

Turn dough onto lightly floured surface; knead 6–8 strokes to mix thoroughly. With floured rolling pin, lightly roll out dough, lifting rolling pin as you near edges to keep dough evenly thick. Roll dough ½-inch thick for high fluffy biscuits, ¼-inch thick for thin crusty ones.

With floured 1- or 2-inch biscuit cutter, cut biscuits, using straight downward motion without twisting. With spatula, place biscuits on ungreased cookie sheet, 1 inch apart for crusty biscuits, nearly touching for soft ones. Press dough trimmings together (don't knead); roll and cut as above until all dough is used. Bake 12–15 minutes, or until golden. If frozen, thaw and reheat in foil in 350° oven 5–10 minutes.

CHEESE BOAT

1 quart cheese dip

The beer-flavored dip is good either heated or at room temperature. It also is a good thing to have on hand for last-minute company. The cheese mixture will remain fresh in the refrigerator for at least four weeks and the rye and pumpernickel cubes can be frozen along with the Bread Boat. This is very hearty food and can stand alone for a smaller gathering of ten. Double the recipe for this menu.

Dip:
- 1 cup beer
- 24 ounces refrigerated Cheddar cheese spread
- 1¼ ounces Roquefort cheese
- 1 small onion
- 2 cloves garlic
- 1 teaspoon Worcestershire sauce
- ½ teaspoon Tabasco

Bread Boat:
- 1 small round loaf rye or pumpernickel bread
- 1 2-pound loaf pumpernickel bread, cut into 1½-inch x 1-inch cubes

Dip: Put dip ingredients into a blender or food processor and blend until smooth. Pour into a quart jar and store in refrigerator. Bring to room temperature when ready to serve.

Bread Boat: Cut a circle 1 inch deep in top of small loaf of rye, leaving a 1-inch rim. Carefully remove circle and scoop out the center of the loaf, leaving a ¾-inch shell. Cut circle and scooped-out bread into cubes to use for dipping. Cut the large loaf of bread into cubes. Cubes may be toasted in oven. Pour cheese dip into boat and surround with bread cubes.

HOT BEEF SPREAD IN CHAFING DISH

Approximately 30 servings

This is a tasty spread that tastes best with plain crackers. Prepare it a day or so before your party and refrigerate. At least double the recipe for a large party.

2 2½-ounce jars (or 1
   4-ounce refrigerated
   package) dried beef,
   chopped
2 8-ounce packages cream
   cheese, at room
   temperature

1½ tablespoons minced onion
1 teaspoon garlic salt
½ teaspoon pepper
2 cups sour cream
4 tablespoons butter, melted
½ teaspoon salt
1 cup chopped pecans

Preheat oven to 325°.

Mix first 6 ingredients and spread in a lightly greased oven-proof chafing dish container or pretty 9-inch quiche dish. Top with a mixture of melted butter, salt, and pecans. Bake for 20 minutes.

ROASTED PECANS

A pleasing touch to any party, can be done way ahead.

4 cups pecan halves
3 tablespoons butter, melted
1 teaspoon salt

Preheat oven to 250°.

Put pecans 1 or 2 layers deep in a baking pan. Roast for 30 minutes, stirring once. Remove from oven and pour melted butter over pecans. Stir with a wooden spoon to coat each nut. Return to the oven for 30–40 minutes, stirring 2 or 3 times. Remove, add salt, stir to coat, and roast 8 minutes more. Store in airtight container.

INDEX

A

Almond lace cookies, easy, 51
Angel food cake
  chocolate mousse, 88
  with strawberry cream, 108-109

APPETIZERS
  broccoli and carrot crudités, 20
  caviar ring, 129
  cheese delights, 141
  cheese en croûte, 16
  cheese puffs, 147
  chicken bites, 139
  crab and cheese melt-aways, 85
  crab cocktail over cream cheese, 20
  crab puffs with phyllo, 67
  cream cheese with cucumber
    relish, 18
  cream cheese surprises, 31
  cucumber, 15
  egg salad pinwheel sandwiches, 140
  French bread, stuffed, 112
  ham roll-ups, 140
  herbed bread sticks, 28
  hot and spicy meatballs, 21
  hot beef spread in chafing dish, 152
  melon balls and prosciutto, 80
  mushrooms filled with crab
    meat, 58
  mushrooms, stuffed, 146
  mushroom turnovers, 142
  oysters and bacon, 18
  party pork balls, 73
  pâté in gelatin, 57
  pecan cheese ball, 104
  pineapple shrimp with dip, 128
  pizza, 146
  quickie bacon roll-ups, 53
  salmon, smoked, and Boursin in
    cucumber cups, 111
  sauerkraut balls, 134
  sausage pizza rounds, 124
  shrimp, marinated, 18
  shrimp balls, 124
  shrimp mold, 85
  shrimp toast, 148
  spinach balls, 21
  spinach cheese squares, 130-131
  tiropetes, 131
  zucchini savories, 148
  see also Brie; Dip
Apricot mold, 126
Artichokes
  casserole, with chicken and
    shrimp, 113
  hearts, breaded, 80
  quiche, 141
Avocado
  mousse, 66
  salad, with oranges and onion, 120

B

Bacon
  and cheese French bread, 120
  oysters and, 18
  quickie roll-ups, 53
Barbecued chicken, 74-75
Beef
  curried dip, 40
  fillet of, with Madeira sauce, 68
  fillet, cold, with sour cream, 106
  flank steak, marinated, on
    buttered rolls, 125
  hot spread in chafing dish, 152
  meatballs, hot and spicy, 21
  steak tartare, 94
  tenderloin with Madeira sauce, 68
  tournedos in puff pastry, 69
Bibb and walnut salad, 63
Biscuits
  cinnamon puffs, 32
  cream cheese surprises, 31
  miniature buttermilk, 150
  quick herbed, 54
  see also Bread
Biscuit tortoni, 83
Blueberry muffins, quick, 32
Blue cheese dressing, 36
Bourbon balls, 29
Bourbon hot dogs, 113
Brandy sauce, 77
Bread
  Camembert French, 76
  cheese and bacon French, 120
  cheese toasts, 44
  French mustard, 101
  garlic, 82

GUIDE TO WEIGHTS AND MEASURES

1 tablespoon = 3 teaspoons		16 tablespoons = 1 cup	
1½ tablespoons = 1 jigger		8 ounces = 1 cup	
2 tablespoons = 1 liquid ounce		1 cup = ½ pint	
4 tablespoons = ¼ cup		2 cups = 1 pint	
5 tablespoons = ⅓ cup		4 cups = 1 quart	
8 tablespoons = ½ cup		4 quarts = 1 gallon	

EQUIVALENTS

1 stick butter = ½ cup = 8 tablespoons = ¼ pound
1 pound granulated white sugar = 2 cups
1 pound packed brown sugar = 2½ cups
1 pound powdered sugar = 3½ cups
1 pound sifted all-purpose flour = 4 cups
1 tablespoon cornstarch = 2 tablespoons flour
1 large package (18.5 ounces) cake mix = 2 cups
1 cup raw, uncooked rice = 3½ cups cooked rice
1 square chocolate = 1 ounce
1 cup nut meats = ¼ pound (approximately)
1 lemon = 3 tablespoons juice (approximately)
2 grated lemon rinds = 2 tablespoons (approximately)
1 cup egg whites = 8–10 whites
1 cup egg yolks = 12–14 yolks
1 cup finely crumbled chocolate sandwich cookies = approximately 12 cookies
1 cup finely crumbled graham crackers = approximately 16 crackers
1 cup finely crumbled saltine crackers = approximately 28 crackers
1 cup finely crumbled vanilla wafers = 34 wafers

SUBSTITUTIONS

¼ teaspoon baking soda + ½ teaspoon cream of tartar = 1 teaspoon baking powder
3½ tablespoons cocoa + 1 tablespoon butter = 1 square chocolate
1⅓ tablespoons vinegar or lemon juice + milk to make 1 cup = 1 cup buttermilk
1 tablespoon vinegar or lemon juice + 1 cup evaporated milk = 1 cup sour cream